Mario Reading was born in Dorset, and brought up in England, Germany, and the South of France. He studied Comparative Literature at the University of East Anglia, where he specialized in French and German literature and translation. He speaks four languages. During a nomadic youth he sold rare books, taught riding in Africa, studied dressage in Vienna, played polo in India, Spain and Dubai, ran a 70-horse polo stables in Gloucestershire, and helped manage his Mexican wife's coffee plantation.

In recent years he has established a worldwide reputation as the leading expert on Nostradamus. He is the author of the best-selling *Nostradamus: The Complete Prophecies for the Future* and also of *Nostradamus: The Good News*. He has recently brought out the ultimate collection of Nostradamus's prophecies in *The Complete Nostradamus* together with an illustrated companion volume entitled *Nostradamus: The Top 100 Prophesies*. The first thriller in his Nostradamus trilogy *The Nostradamus Prophecies*, was an international bestseller in 36 countries. The second volume, *The Mayan Codex* appeared in 2010, with the concluding part due out in 2011. Mario has appeared in a number of documentaries on Nostradamus for, amongst others, the Discovery Channel, the National Geographic Channel, and the History Channel.

By the same author

Non-Fiction
The Complete Prophecies of Nostradamus
Nostradamus: The Top 100 Prophecies
Nostradamus: The Complete Prophecies for the Future
Nostradamus: The Good News
The Watkins Dictionary of Dreams
The Dictionary of Cinema
The Movie Companion

Fiction
The Nostradamus Prophecies
The Mayan Codex
The Music-Makers

Please return/renew this item by the last date shown.

To renew this item, call **0845 0020777** (automated)
or visit **www.librarieswest.org.uk**

Borrower number and PIN required.

Libraries**West**

V I   N G

This edition first published in the UK and USA 2011 by
Watkins Publishing, Sixth Floor, Castle House,
75–76 Wells Street, London W1T 3QH

1 3 5 7 9 10 8 6 4 2

Designed and typeset by Jerry Goldie
Printed and bound by Imago in China

British Library Cataloguing-in-Publication Data Available

Library of Congress Cataloging-in-Publication Data Available

ISBN: 978-1-907486-67-8

www.watkinspublishing.co.uk

Distributed in the USA and Canada by Sterling Publishing Co., Inc.
387 Park Avenue South, New York, NY 10016-8810

For information about custom editions, special sales, premium and
corporate purchases, please contact Sterling Special Sales
Department at 800-805-5489 or specialsales@sterlingpub.com

CONTENTS

From Ben Jonson's *Bartholomew Fair* (1614)

Zeal-of-the-land Busy [a Puritan hypocrite]: 'Look not toward them, harken not: the place is Smithfield, or the Field of Smiths, the Grove of Hobby-horses and Trinkets, the Wares are the Wares of Devils. And the whole Fair is the Shop of Satan! They are Hooks and Baits, very Baits, that are hung out on every side, to catch you, and to hold you, as it were, by the Gills, and by the Nostrils, as the Fisher doth: Therefore you must not look nor turn toward them – The Heathen man could stop his Ears with Wax against the Harlot o' the Sea: Do you the like with your Fingers against the Bells o' the Beast.'

ACT III SCENE II

Lanthorn Leatherhead [a cleverly ridiculed Inigo Jones, who produced stage effects for some of Jonson's *Masques*]: 'Or what do you say to a Drum, Sir?'

Busy: 'It is the broken Belly of the Beast, and thy Bellows there are his Lungs, and these Pipes are his Throat, those Feathers are of his Tail, and thy Rattles the gnashing of his Teeth.'

ACT III SCENE VI

He said to me, 'John, John, why do you doubt, or why are you afraid? You are not unfamiliar with this image, are you? – that is, do not be timid! – I am the one who is with you always. I am the Father, I am the Mother, I am the Son. I am the undefiled and incorruptible one. Now I have come to teach you what is and what was and what will come to pass, that you may know the things which are not revealed and those which are revealed, and to teach you concerning the unwavering race of the perfect Man. Now, therefore, lift up your face, that you may receive the things that I shall teach you today, and may tell them to your fellow spirits who are from the unwavering race of the perfect Man.'

From The Apocryphon of John (Found at Nag Hammadi in 1945, and translated by Frederik Wisse)

For my brother, Rainer Rummel,
and my grandmother, Else Priester

ACKNOWLEDGEMENTS

As has become my wont in recent years, I'd like to thank a number of people who have helped with this book's journey from prolepsis to printer. This is clearly the only way open to me of avoiding the trap so succinctly described by Luc de Clapiers, Marquis de Vauvenargues, who wrote: *C'est un grand signe de mediocrité, de louer toujours modérément* ('To be niggard in one's praise of others is a sure sign of mediocrity in oneself'). Thanks must go firstly to my friend and long-time editor, Michael Mann, for whom de Vauvenargues no doubt intended the following axiom (which his notional subject, I should add, has fully taken to heart): *Apprenons à subordonner les petits intérêts aux grands, et faisons généreusement tout le bien qui tente nos coeurs: on ne peut être dupe d'aucune vertu* ('Learn to overrule minor interests in favour of great ones, and generously do all the good the heart prompts; a man is never injured by acting virtuously'). To Shelagh Boyd, friend and long-time copy-editor, *a chaque saint son cierge* ('to each saint his candle' – in other words 'honour to whom honour is due'). To my friend and agent, Oliver Munson, perfectly described by Voltaire's wise dictum: *C'est par le caractère, et non par l'esprit, que l'on fait fortune* ('Men make fortune by their mettle, not their wits'). And finally to Claudia, my wife, friend, and confidante, whom Sainte-Foix described to perfection in the following: *La femme a un sourire pour toutes les joies, une larme pour toutes les douleurs, une consolation pour toutes les misères, une excuse pour toutes les fautes, une prière pour toutes les infortunes, un encouragement pour toutes les espérances* ('Woman has a smile for every joy, a tear for every grief, consolation for all misery, excuses for all faults, a prayer for misfortune, and encouragement for all hopes').

INTRODUCTION

This is the very first time in publishing history that all of Nostradamus's quatrains relating exclusively to those he considered to be the three Antichrists – namely Napoleon Bonaparte, Adolf Hitler, and the 'One Still To Come' – have been brought together in one book. The rationale behind the decision to publish was an easy one. It consisted of a series of 'what ifs'.

For instance, what if all the extant information on the Antichrists, revealed by the cracking of the index date codes in my three previous Nostradamus books, was gathered together and laid before my readers? What might they learn? What might all the Antichrist quatrains – seen in toto and, even more crucially, outside their usual context – show? And wouldn't this be the ideal way to allow people to make up their own minds about Nostradamus's vision for the coming apocalypse, rather than via the usual pre-digested pap promulgated by a plethora of not entirely disinterested eschatologists, and in which the grinding of a multitude of axes invariably drowns out anything that passes for common sense? The answer was obvious. But it also begged a number of important questions.

Did Nostradamus see the world we live in as inevitably doomed? Did he believe, like that great novelist of the post-apocalypse, Cormac McCarthy, that:

> ...there's no such thing as life without bloodshed. The notion that the species can be improved in

some way, that everyone could live in harmony, is a really dangerous idea. Those who are afflicted with this notion are the first ones to give up their souls, their freedom. Your desire that it be that way will enslave you and make your life vacuous.

Or did he believe that humanity could learn from its historical mistakes and rectify matters before they came to an apocalyptic head? And why did Nostradamus decide that there were three Antichrists, and not the one apparently foretold in Revelation? Would the prophesied arrival of the third and final Antichrist betoken Armageddon and the End of Days, or would it simply mark a Great Change – something along the lines of what the Mayans are suggesting for 21 December 2012, when the Long Count Calendar and the Cycle of Nine Hells are both expected to conclude at roughly the same time?

My first instinct was, and still is, that the answer is contained within the quatrains – one has only to gather them together and ask the right questions. Sir Galahad – the knightly embodiment of Jesus in the Arthurian legends – followed a similar path when he finally learned that the true question needed to unlock the secrets of the Holy Grail was not the obvious 'What are you?', but rather the infinitely more noumenal 'How can I serve you?' Faith, in other words, and not curiosity, is the prerequisite.

The process of choice was, in and of itself, an interesting one. My first criterion was simply to check through my own *The Complete Prophecies Of Nostradamus* (Watkins 2009) to see which historical personages Nostradamus wrote about the most. Would they be largely destructive or benevolent? Would they grace the world with their presence, or disgrace it? The list I came up with was a fascinating one, with perpetrators of evil, destruction, and bad faith securing all three of the top places.

Far and away the top runner in terms of numbers was Napoleon Bonaparte, with 47 quatrains to his name – that's five per cent out of Nostradamus's grand total of 942 quatrains. An incredible figure, surely, given that Nostradamus was writing 250 years before the revolutionary events he describes with such uncanny accuracy.

Second in line was Adolf Hitler, with 30 quatrains to his name – Nostradamus was writing a full 380 years before Adolf Hitler's seemingly inexorable rise to power, making the factual accuracy and concentrated historical nous contained in his Hitler quatrains an even more astonishing achievement.

Adolf Hitler's total is closely mirrored by that of Nostradamus's Third Antichrist personification – the mysterious and unnamed stranger we shall call the 'One Still To Come' – to whom Nostradamus dedicates an extraordinary 36 quatrains. This time the seer was writing about events due to occur more than 600 years after his own death, thereby stretching to its very limit the 700-year boundary he appears to have imposed on himself.

So between them Nostradamus's three Antichrists notch up more than 100 out of his grand total of 942 published quatrains – a significant preponderance, I trust you'll agree.

When placed alongside the 100 Antichrist quatrains, the 5 or so quatrains apiece that Nostradamus dedicates to Henri II, Henri IV, Philip II, Charles I, Marie de Medici, Louis XIII, Louis XIV, Cardinal Richelieu, and Benito Mussolini, *inter alia*, pale into insignificance. True, he concentrates considerable attention, and a considerable number of quatrains, on the French Wars of Religion, the Lutheran Heresy, and the Ottoman Empire, but these are generalized quatrains, and do not refer to any specific Antichrist. They are simply part of the vast historical panorama that Nostradamus appears to have had at his fingertips.

No. Three specific historical figures get all his attention, and in my chapters entitled 'The Concept of the Antichrist' and 'Nostradamus's Antichrists', I attempt to tease out why. In addition I have constructed timelines relating to each of Nostradamus's three Antichrists, and I finish up with a Conclusion summarizing what I have found.

I trust that, by the end of this sequence, my readers will feel that the journey they have undertaken has been worth the effort, and that their understanding of Nostradamian process has been concomitantly enriched.

Biographical Preamble

The idea that any historian or biographer is 'right', or is creating more than yet another believable and interesting myth to overlay and influence an already existing myth, is fundamentally absurd. Few people can even describe the day that has just passed accurately – let alone decades, if not centuries, before their own time. No, what historians and biographers are giving us is an informed opinion, and a vastly subjective one at that, dependent on the often sparse material that has been left, frequently as a result of random historical happenstance, and to which they inevitably ascribe – because they have a vested interest in so doing – far too much significance.

The winners in history usually hide what is inconvenient to

them, or manipulate the truth to suit the scale of their ambitions, and the losers bleat, or are written out of history altogether (Mithraism being but one obvious example) – that is, after all, human nature. When losers do out-survive those they feel have done them (or their cabal) wrong, as often as not they try to rewrite history the better to reinforce their feelings of outrage and despair – that too is human nature. All history is therefore fiction disguised as fact, but actually representing the historians' best shot at an almost-truth. It is for exactly this reason that apocryphal stories, hearsay, and scandal are potentially just as historically relevant as (purported) dry facts, government documents (a likely story), and contemporary commentaries (untarnished, of course, by even the merest hint of vainglory or rodomontade!).

Wars have been fought over lesser issues than the details of Nostradamus's alleged biography. Scholars have been declaring that only they know the true story from as far back as the late 16th century, and their descendants still continue to do so today (and with equal impunity). So little is actually known about Nostradamus's life, however, that some of the more apocryphal stories, often stemming from a century or so after his death, become important pointers in themselves – not so much to the 'real life' (as if anyone is capable of teasing that out from the mass of obfuscation, forgery, and hearsay that underlies much Nostradamus scholarship) as to the life he ought to have led, given the reality of his influence.

Anyway, here is a short biographical note that does not purport to be the exact truth (what can?) so much as to coalesce both given, disputed, and established facts into some sort of sensible (if inevitably fallible) order.

BIOGRAPHICAL NOTE

The medieval France *profonde* into which Michel de Nostredame (1503-66) was born encompassed a mass of different sects, tribes, and communities, but with no truly effective central government. Villagers from the Pyrenees or from deepest Provence, for instance, might never have heard of Paris, nor would they have understood Parisian French if it were spoken to them – faces, manners, and even language varied alarmingly according to the contours of the valleys in which people lived.

Isolated communities were surrounded by a ripple-effect of further enclaves, mini-fiefdoms, clan centres (with bells delineating tribal territories), and racial diversifications, dating all the way back to pre-history – a charivari that remained in place well into the 19th century, with distant echoes of its dying fall still reverberating today.

Few French people had ever seen a map of France. Fewer still were aware of French history as a definable, ongoing process. Of the total population, 98 per cent were deemed to be Catholic, it is true, but with marked variations in religious practice. Local priests competed with quacks, witches, healers, simple-mongers, and weather merchants for the hearts and souls of their parish. Before the French Revolution (1789–99), the word 'France' was merely used to describe a truncated area in and around Paris. In Provence, someone from the north might be termed a *Franciot* or *Franchiman*, and the Provençal-born and Francoprovençal-speaking Nostradamus would most probably have grown up with a quasi-atavistic mistrust of both the royal government and its motivations (largely on account of a cultural and linguistic bifurcation that was only really addressed by the Abbé

Henri Grégoire at the time of the 1793–94 Reign of Terror).

For Nostradamus, it must be remembered, was both a committed, mainstream Catholic, and an ethnic – and therefore potentially ostracizable – Jew. If that sounds like a paradox, it wasn't perceived as such in a 16th-century France dedicated to both God, in the form of the Inquisition, and Mammon, in the form of the pillaging of others' property for reasons of ecclesiastical expediency. For 30 years, under the reign of Good King René, the Jews of Provence had been accorded the free practice of their religion, but all that ended with René's death in 1480, a date which unfortunately coincided with the inception of the Spanish Inquisition.

By the time of Nostradamus's birth in 1503, most prominent Jews had prudently converted to a pragmatic form of Catholicism, thanks to the edicts of, respectively, Charles VIII in 1488, and Louis XII in 1501. This didn't prevent the French Crown from occasionally plundering their possessions, but it did offer them a measure of protection in a country suddenly rife with religious intolerance and paranoia. So the infant Michel de Nostredame found himself both uncircumcised (the penalty for which, under Levitical law, is ostracism from the congregation of Israel), and baptized according to the Christian rite, whilst retaining, in the form of his maternal great-grandfather, Jean de Saint-Rémy, an intimate access to the Jewish chain of tradition, the *Schalscheleth Ha-Kabbalah*, which was to stand him in very good stead in his later incarnation as a diviner and scryer.

As a result of this upbringing, Nostradamus almost certainly dabbled in magic, and very certainly in mysticism and the kabbalah, which encapsulated the Jewish search for new wisdom in a creative synthesis between the mythologies of ancient Egypt, ancient Greece, Assyrian astrology, Babylonian magic, Arabian divination, Platonic philosophy, and Gnosticism (Gershom Scholem, in his *Major Trends In Jewish Mysticism* writes that 'it can be taken as certain that...ancient writings, with Gnostic excerpts written in Hebrew, made their way from the East to Provence...to become one of the chief influences which shaped the theosophy of the thirteenth-century kabbalists.').

The secretive and mystical nature of the kabbalah, therefore, would have provided a much-needed escape from the grim realities of Jewish life in an Inquisitorial Europe, and a much-needed panacea in the face of the forcible conversions that followed René's death. By pure chance, Nostradamus's native town of St-Rémy was the perfect place to study the kabbalah, as Provence was generally acknowledged as home to the earliest kabbalistic community in France. Paradoxically, perhaps, Nostradamus, as well as being a kabbalist, an alchemist, and a Talmudist, was also a fervent adherent to Catholic doctrine throughout his life, and would certainly not have been accepted at Avignon University (not then a part of France) had he not been sincere in these assertions, and in his excoriation of the near ubiquitous Lutheran heresy. He later enrolled, again without problem, at the venerable University of Montpellier (founded in 1220) in order to study medicine – a wise move, as Montpellier possessed, without doubt, the greatest school of medicine of those times.

After matriculating from Montpellier (from which he had briefly been expelled on 3 October 1529, for the alleged crime of having practised as an apothecary, before being readmitted, third time lucky, on 23 October that same year) – and following hard upon an invigilation process that would have been conducted in the medieval manner of a formal dispute between the student and the teaching staff, rather than merely by written examination – Nostradamus was plunged straight into the treatment of an outbreak of the plague.

Encumbered by the usual paraphernalia worn by medical practitioners during such crises (Irish physician Neil O'Glacan (1590–1655), in his *Tractatus de Peste* (Toulouse 1629), describes plague doctors as wearing long leather gowns stained with many different coloured powders, gauntlets, leather masks with glass protection for the eyes, and a long sponge-filled beak imbrued with fumigants for the nose), Nostradamus struck out into entirely new territory with his invention of a purifying powder (his 'rose pill'), which, we are led to believe, inspired an entirely untypical confidence in his patients. As a direct consequence of this experience, Nostradamus became something of an authority on the plague, a talent that was sorely tested when plague struck, once again, during his tenure as a doctor at Agen, killing his young wife and their two children. As a result, Nostradamus not only suffered from the usual criticism of 'Physician, heal thyself', but was also sued by the distraught family of his wife for the return of her dowry.

Traumatized by his loss, Nostradamus took to the road, and travelled through many parts of France, Italy, and Sicily, before finally settling in Salon de Provence. There, at the age of 44, he met a widow, Anne Ponsarde Gemelle (*gemellus* implies a twin in Latin), whom he married on 11 November 1547. They moved into a house on the Rue Ferreiraux (now known as Rue Nostradamus), and Nostradamus, in considerable demand by this time, not least for his sovereign remedies, continued his travels.

It was during this period that, thanks to his meetings with

apothecaries, physicians and magicians, he first began to suspect that he had the gift of prophecy and second sight. He was not the only one. Under the reign of the 13 Valois kings, it was estimated that there were upwards of 30,000 astrologers, sorcerers, alchemists, and prophets practising in Paris alone, and it is to Nostradamus's credit, and to that of his art, that he rose, inexorably, to the top of a very crowded tree.

Three years after the publication of his *Traité Des Fardemens* in 1552 (an *à la mode* treatise on unguents, jams and preserves of all kinds), Nostradamus followed up – rather tentatively, it must be said – with the first edition of his famous *Centuries* (1555), fearing, according to his pupil, Jean Aymes de Chavigny, both castigation and mockery. The 353 quatrains, to just about everybody's surprise, including that of Nostradamus, were a sensation. Summoned to Paris by Henri II's queen, Catherine de Medici, barely a year after publication, Nostradamus returned to Salon a rich man, having discovered, the hard way, that private practice (the casting of personal horoscopes and the alleviation of courtiers' ailments) was considerably more remunerative, and a good deal less precarious, than celebrity stargazing. Nostradamus continued to advise the queen, however, not least because she protected him, in some measure, from falling foul of the religious authorities for blasphemy, while her regal favour afforded him a much-appreciated kudos and the promise of a steady income.

Nostradamus's career really took off with his extraordinary series of quatrains depicting the accidental death, in a joust, of King Henri II of France. This uncannily accurate series of five quatrains cemented Nostradamus's reputation with Catherine de Medici, and ensured him an uninterrupted income stream from enthusiastic clients for the rest of his life.

In a rare but salutary bout of discretion, Nostradamus disguised the true dates of the king's death, knowing that regicide – or even the suspicion of regicide – carried an exemplary and excruciating series of publicly witnessed tortures. The fact that Nostradamus's fears for the king's life were seconded by Luca Gaurico, the court astrologer, afforded him further credence. That they were also convenient to the queen, who wished to prevent her husband from following certain courses of action she found uncongenial, merely served to endear Nostradamus further to her heart.

The full sequence of five quatrains follows below, for I believe it further illustrates Nostradamus's extraordinary pre-cognitive capacity, and may go some little way towards persuading readers that Nostradamus's later Antichrist quatrains were also written in the utmost good faith.

Death of King Henri II of France I

10 July 1559
Nostradamus's Index Date: 35
Century Number: I

Le lion jeune le vieux surmontera,
En champ bellique par singulier duelle:
Dans caige d'or les yeux lui crevera,
Deux classes une, puis mourir, mort cruelle.

The young lion will overcome the old one
Hand to hand, on the field of combat
His eyes will burst in their golden helmet
Two breaks in one, followed by a merciless death.

Published a full three years before the fateful death it foretold, this is the famous quatrain detailing the death, in a joust, of King Henri II of France. Despite repeated warnings from both Nostradamus, his queen, and his Italian court astrologer, Luca Gaurico, the virile 41-year-old king insisted on taking an active part in the three-day tournament arranged to celebrate the double marriages of his sister, Marguerite, to the Duke of Savoy, and of his eldest daughter, Elizabeth, to King Philip II of Spain, as agreed in the Treaty of Cateau-Cambrésis.

Galvanized by his success in the first two days of the jousting, Henri challenged Gabriel de Lorges, Count of Montgomery, and captain of his Scottish Guard, to ritual single combat on the third and final day of the tournament. They duly exchanged lances, leading to a tie. But Henri was not satisfied – he insisted on a second bout. Montgomery havered. The king, despite the entreaties of his wife, stood on his rights as a combatant. The joust took place. At the very last moment, sensing disaster, the 35-year-old Montgomery tried to avoid the king's person, but his lance caught on the lip of Henri's helmet, splintering on his visor, and entering the king's right orbit and temple, just above the right eye.

Despite prompt treatment by Master Surgeon Ambroise Paré, and Philip II's great anatomist, Andreas Vesalius, Henri began to succumb to cerebral infection and cerebral trauma.

Desperate to find a remedy for her husband's injury, his queen, Catherine de Medici, ordered four criminals to be beheaded, and broken truncheons to be forced into their right eyes 'at an appropriate angle' in order to ascertain the full extent of the king's wound. The cerebral trauma, however, had now caused Henri's left eye to become grotesquely swollen, even further mirroring Nostradamus's original prediction. Four days after the joust, and despite the best efforts of his wife and surgeons, the king became feverish, quickly followed by paralysis of the right side and lengthy convulsions. Henri died an agonizing death six days later, on 10 July 1559. He was buried in a cadaver tomb at the Basilica of St Denis, and his premature death undoubtedly changed the course of French and European history.

The crestfallen Montgomery, pardoned by the king on his deathbed, succumbed to the widowed queen's disfavour a full 15 years after her husband's death. That, too, was predicted by Nostradamus, in quatrain 3/30: 1530–74 (Gabriel de Montgomery, Seigneur de Lorges – *see* my *The Complete Prophecies of Nostradamus*) – right down to the armed men who hurried him to the Conciergerie prison, where this belated Protestant convert and survivor of the massacre of the Huguenots was finally put to death.

Summary

Refusing to listen to Nostradamus's repeated warnings that he would die in a joust, macho King Henri II of France is fatally injured during a tournament to celebrate the joint marriages of his daughter and sister, and the peace treaty of Cateau-Cambrésis. Henri's death was good news for Spain, England, Italy and Austria, and particularly good news for Nostradamus, whose divinatory fame it secured.

Death of King Henri II of France II

Nostradamus's Index Date: 73
Century Number: 8

Soldat barbare le grand Roy frappera,
Injustement non eslongné de mort,
L'avare mere du fait cause sera
Coniurateur & regne en grand remort.

A barbarous soldier will strike against the king
Unjustly, not far away from death
The greedy one, mother of the deed, will have caused it
Both conspirator and kingdom lament what they have done.

PREDICTION

This quatrain must be read in conjunction with 1/35 – 1559 [Death of King Henri II Of France I], for it would appear to be yet another disguised reference to the accidental killing, in a friendly joust, of that unlucky monarch. The 'barbarous soldier' was Gabriel de Montgomery, Seigneur de Lorges, a hereditary lieutenant in the king's Scottish Guard, and responsible for the king's death. The simple fact of Montgomery's inadvertently-splintered lance entering the king's visor was to toll the funerary knell for the entire House of Valois, which petered out 30 years later.

SUMMARY

A disguised quatrain bemoaning the untimely death of France's King Henri II, husband of Nostradamus's benefactress, Catherine de Medici.

Death of King Henri II of France III

Nostradamus's Index Date: 55
Century Number: 3

En l'an qu'un oeil en France regnera,
La court sera à un bien fascheux trouble:
Le grand de Bloys son ami tuera,
Le regne mis en mal & doubte double.

In the year when a one-eyed man reigns in France
The court will be greatly troubled
The great one of Blois will kill his friend
The reign struck by evil and double doubt.

PREDICTION

The index date is four years out here, as King Henri II lost his
eye in a joust in 1559 [*see* 1/35 – 1559: Death of King Henri II of
France I, and 8/73 – 1559: Death of King Henri II of France II],
and died ten days later. In this particular instance, however,
Nostradamus might have muddied the waters on purpose – just
as he was to do in the other quatrains of the Henri II series – as
too accurate a prediction of such earth-shattering events might
have risked the wrath of the Inquisition (in the sense of
implying a human prerogation of God's powers). The third and
fourth lines of the quatrain move to the more distant future,
and describe the eventual downfall of the Valois line – for
Henri's third son, Henri III ('the great one of Blois'), went on
to have his old friend and rival, Henri, Duc de Guise, assassinated in 1588. This effectively split the pro-Catholic forces into

two disparate groupings ('double doubt'), and paved the way
for the dying out of the Valois line in favour of the Bourbons.

SUMMARY

The one-eyed man is King Henri II, and his death in a friendly
joust indirectly heralded the end of the Valois line.

Death of King Henri II of France IV

Nostradamus's Index Date: 24
Century Number: 8

Le lieutenant à l'entrée de l'huys,
Assommera la grand de Parpignan,
En se cuidant sauluer à Montpertuis.
Sera deceu bastard de Lusignan.

The lieutenant at the doorway
Will fell the great man of Perpignan
Thinking himself welcomed at Montpertuis
He will be deceived by the bastard of Lusignan.

PREDICTION

All the places mentioned are in France, but Perpignan is down
by the Catalan border, and Lusignan is up near Poitiers, while
Mont Pertuis probably refers to the mountainous area around
Le Pertuis in the Haute-Loire – frankly, the places could hardly
be farther apart, nor more disparate in terms of medieval
ownership. France's most famous 'lieutenant who felled a great

man' is undoubtedly Gabriel, Comte de Montgomery, who was a lieutenant in Henri II of France's Scottish Guard when he had the misfortune to fell the king in a joust, thanks to a shattered lance. The king died ten days later.

Summary

A further possible reference to Gabriel de Montgomery, unwitting killer of King Henri II of France.

Death of King Henri II of France V

Nostradamus's Index Date: 70
Century Number: 10

L'oeil par obiect fera telle excroissance,
Tant & ardente que tumbera la neige,
Champ arrousé viendra en descroissance,
Que le primat succumbera à Regne.

The eye will swell because of a foreign object
So much and so burning that the snow will fall
The field will be sprayed so that nothing will grow
The first one in the kingdom will succumb.

Prediction

This is clearly another King Henri II quatrain, with its index date, as always with Henri II quatrains, disguised. The splintered lance that entered Henri's temple did indeed cause his 'eye to swell' dramatically, affording him excruciating pain for the ten days he continued living [*see* 1/35, 8/73, 3/55 and 8/24 – 1559: Death of King Henri II of France I–IV]. In line three's telling image, Nostradamus appears to be suggesting that the tourney field upon which the king was mortally injured might be sown or 'sprayed' with salt, so that nothing further can grow on it.

SUMMARY

An accurate and detailed quatrain bringing to an end the brilliant series of verses Nostradamus dedicates to the accidental death of King Henri II.

In terms of the apparent dangers Nostradamus faced from the Inquisition, it is important to draw a distinction, just as Alexander of Hales (1183–1245) did, between the two principal, although different, forms of magic. Namely *divination* (from the Latin *divinitas*, meaning the godhead, or the divine nature), which was seen as High Magic; and *maleficum* or evil-doing (from the Latin *maleficus*, meaning hurtful or mischievous), which, in the Middle Ages, was the word coined to represent Low Magic. Low Magic was designed for instant gratification – the equivalent, in magical terms, of a caffeine hit. It might span the ritual burning of hair, the spearing of wax dolls, or sacrificial offerings leading to fruitful crops or the emergence of rain after a long dry spell. High Magic incorporated astrology and alchemy, and was built on a firm philosophical foundation, deriving as much from Pythagoras as it did from the Persian Magi, Gnosticism, or Neo-Platonism. Both were thus categorically different in origin, with Low Magic drawing much of its motive power from Aristotelianism. High Magic was therefore a subject of justifiable study, and if not quite 'nice', at least intellectually acceptable. Low Magic was considered akin to witchcraft.

Nostradamus, needless to say, was a High Magic figure, taking his cue from the *Corpus Hermeticum*, a magical treatise believed, in medieval times, to be of the highest antiquity, but later proved by Isaac Casaubon (no relation, beyond the obvious, to George Eliot's fictional *Middlemarch* antihero) to have been composed circa the 2nd or 3rd century AD – Casaubon's opinion carried great weight, as, in his day (1559–1614) he was considered, alongside the Agen-born Joseph Scaliger, to be the most learned man in Europe.

Nostradamus's adherence to High Magic, therefore, provided him with considerable protection from Inquisitorial inquiry, and, alongside his support from the queen, made it even more likely that he did not have either the need or the motivation to hide or codify his index dates (except in the aforementioned extreme circumstances, when they dealt with the death of living kings). This High Magic itinerary of Nostradamus's also tallies with his pedagogical intentions – for he truly believed that mankind was subject to an overweening fate, and that nothing in history occurred as the result of accident. Everything was either intended or preprogrammed, and as such could be teased out through scrying, divination, necromancy, hydromancy, chiromancy, astrology, dream interpretation, the study of ancient texts, numerology, alchemy, the kabbalah, hermetic inference, and the manipulation of the fundamental chemical composition of inanimate objects. With each step in the divinatory cycle, the adept was led to a higher level of understanding, which culminated in a process of mental and spiritual purification leading to absolute clarity of thought. Such a spiritual catharsis allowed the adept access to hidden truths that, with the best possible of intentions, he would then lay before the world to make of it what it willed.

Such apparent self-glorification was frowned on by the religious community, but it wasn't, for the most part, considered witchcraft, and its zealots were allowed to practise, to all intents and purposes, unmolested. However, magic was, most definitely, anti-clerical, in the sense that many of its adherents believed that they had been specifically chosen to express God's intentions, rather than simply to respond to them, as a priest or a true believer would. To this extent alone was Nostradamus in danger, and he retorted to such allegations by making it clear, on numerous occasions, that he did not feel himself to be a consciously chosen vessel, but merely a random one, selected by happenstance.

Consciously chosen vessel or not, the summit of Nostradamus's stratospherical celebrity career came during a royal visit to Salon itself, in 1564, by the boy king, Charles IX (who would later, at his dominant mother's instigation, approve the St Bartholomew's Day Massacre). Catherine invited Nostradamus and his family to a private visit at the royal apartments, and then to a further consultation, where she asked him to cast the horoscope of her youngest son, the Duke of Anjou. Nostradamus was more interested in the young Henri de Navarre, however, and even investigated the ten-year-old child whilst he was sleeping, predicting that he would eventually inherit all of France.

Thanks to the evidence contained in Nostradamus's last will and testament, we know that he must have been very well paid for his troubles, a factor that must have provided him with considerable comfort during his two declining years, for, assailed by gout, arthritis, and a heart condition that even his own sovereign remedies failed to alleviate, he finally succumbed on 2 July 1566, in exactly the fashion he had predicted for himself.

THE CONCEPT OF
THE ANTICHRIST

For more than two millennia the name of the Antichrist has either titivated the public imagination, or frozen it in its tracks with fear. It has been used both as a stick to beat non-believers with, and as a goad to gee up the recalcitrant. It has been waved over faithless children as a bogeyman, and over freethinkers as an 'objective correlative' to free thought.

T S Eliot explained the concept of the 'objective correlative' perfectly in his *The Sacred Wood* (1920), whilst discussing the problems inherent in William Shakespeare's *Hamlet*:

> The only way of expressing emotion in the form of art is by finding an 'objective correlative'; in other words, a set of objects, a situation, a chain of events which shall be the formula of that particular emotion; such that when the external facts, which must terminate in sensory experience, are given, the emotion is immediately evoked.

The concept of the Antichrist originated in Jewish eschatology, with the original model probably being Antiochus IV Epiphanes (215–164 BC), persecutor of the Jews, with subsidiary models represented by the 'undead' Nero (Nero *redivivus* – people expected him to pop up again many decades, if not centuries, after his death), Pompey, Herod the Great, and Caligula. These were, in turn, imbrued with Iranian dualism, as recounted in the final great conflict between Auramazda and Ahriman, and Babylonian end-myths, as described in the last great battle of the supreme god Marduk with the dragon of chaos, Tiamāt.

The Christians then hijacked the concept of the Antichrist from the Jews, making of it the perfect Eliotonian 'objective correlative' – the only word that needs to be changed in Eliot's explanation of the term is the word 'art' into 'faith'. The Johannine Antichrist, achieved this to perfection. He is the necessary embodiment of an evil that, by its very presence, also suggests good. If God sends his only son, Jesus Christ, into the world to save it (goes the logic), then Satan, God's necessary mirror image, would also need to send down a counterpart to Jesus Christ to act as *his* representative. This person is the Antichrist.

The medieval Catholic scholastic community tended to fall into two distinct camps over the issue. Preterist eschatologists believed that the prophecies of the Antichrist had been fulfilled before the popes ruled in Rome, i.e. in the first century after Jesus Christ's birth – while futurist eschatologists believed that the Antichrist would appear at some as yet to be determined time in the future, when he would rule the world for a period of three and a half years.

It is an established fact that each nation and religion forged the Antichrists that it felt it deserved. The French, the Spanish, and the Italians, *ergo* the principal Roman Catholic powers, tended to view English Protestant monarchs such as Henry VIII and Elizabeth I as Antichristian, and when this started to pall, scholars such as Tomaso Malvenda (1566–1628), Roberto

Bellarmino (1542–1621), Francisco Ribeira (1537–91) and Luis de Alcazar (1554–1613) encouraged both the papacy and the Catholic ascendancy to turn its attention to the Jews – for medieval tradition had it that the Antichrist would one day be born a Jew, in Babylon, and stemming from the tribe of Dan, before going on to be destroyed by God on or around Mount Olivet.

This largely apocryphal theory would appear to stem from such early Christian sources as Hippolytus (circa 202) and St Cyril of Jerusalem (315–86), and was later to be promulgated by such otherwise estimable figures as St Albertus Magnus (1206–80), St Thomas Aquinas (1225–74), Joachim of Fiore (1135–1202) (*Expo sitio in Apocalipsim*), and Adso, Abbot of the Cluniac Monastery of Moutier-en-Der, who died in 992 whilst on a pilgrimage to Jerusalem, and whose tractate, *De Ortu et Tempore Antichristi*, was to have a long-lasting influence on the arguably inherent anti-Semitism of the Catholic Church. Such unthinking anti-Semitism was to stretch out in a bell curve right through the Middle Ages, the Enlightenment, and the Victorian era, to culminate in such trumped-up nonsenses as the 1905 *Protocols of Zion*, which would, in turn, hasten the coming of the extremes of Hitlerian Germany.

And if it wasn't the Jews who were threatening Christian hegemony, it was the Turk. Given the depredations visited upon Mediterranean shipping over a period of 500 years by the Barbary Pirates – acting, for the most part, it has to be said, under the aegis of the Ottoman Empire – it is hardly surprising that the Mediterranean powers (including, unsurprisingly, the Greeks), stung by Protestant Europe's avocation that the papacy housed the Antichrist, would not project, like a bullied child saying 'ya ya with knobs on', the identical concept onto another, equal irritant.

But how could a Turk, who was, by default, a non-Christian, be an Antichrist? The answer to that conundrum might well give us the key to the Jewish/Catholic Nostradamus's choice for his three Antichrists.

In a final, ironical twist to the tale, Islamic Millenarian doctrine developed its very own Antichrist figure in Djadjdjal, from the Hadith of Nawwas ibn Sam'an – this time aimed at European colonizers of the African sub-continent. Djadjdjal would be a frizzy-haired young man, small of stature. He would walk with his heels apart, he would be blind in one eye, he would enter all towns and villages on earth – except Mecca and Medina – and sow terror and corruption.

What goes around must, of necessity, come around. Or so it seems.

Paul the Apostle is predictably categorical about the impending situation in II Thessalonians 2: 3–4 (King James Version):

> Let no man deceive you by any means: for *that day shall not come*, except there come a falling away first, and that man of sin be revealed, the son of perdition: Who opposeth and exalteth himself above all that is called God, or that is worshipped: so that he as God sitteth in the temple of God, shewing himself that he is God.

A literal, word-by-word translation from the original Greek would go as follows:

No one should seduce you in any manner; because
it will not come unless the apostasy comes first
and reveals the man of lawlessness, the son of
destruction, the lying one who lifts himself up
over God and other objects of reverence, and who
sits down as a God in the divine habitation of
God, showing himself off that he is God.

Most commentators, by and large, have gone with the concept
of the Antichrist as one single person or being, encapsulating
within himself – for he is invariably a 'he' – all that is anti-
Christian, anti-theist, and anti-establishment. In other words,
everything that threatened the fundamental status quo of the
established Christian world. When a new sect appeared, well, it
was led by the Antichrist. When doubts were raised about the
exact degree of moral perfection pertaining to the Church's
activities, well, the caviller was imbrued with the lifeblood of
the Antichrist.

When Martin Luther posted his 95 Theses on the front door
of the *Schlosskirche* at Wittenberg on 31 October 1517, he cleverly
turned this argument back onto the Church politic by attacking
the promulgation of pardons and indulgences (i.e. the full or
partial remission of temporal punishment via confession,
expiation, or in the case of the Church in Luther's time, by tariff
penances, donations, and the sale of indulgences by professional
pardoners in return for so-called 'perpetual remission') by ques-
tioning, particularly given Pope Leo X's immense personal
wealth, why such a holy man did not simply undertake to
finance the long-mooted renovation of St Peter's Basilica in
Rome out of his own pocket, rather than via the stinging of the

poor in return for trumped-up salvatory promises.

Luther's Thesis 86 has this to say on the subject: 'Again: Why does not the pope, whose wealth is today greater than the riches of the richest, build just this one church of St Peter with his own money, rather than with the money of poor believers?'

Luther's underlying message was clear. If the pope claimed that he held carte blanche to promulgate any and every whim, and to run the Holy Mother Church in any way that he saw fit, using, as his pretext, that he was Jesus Christ's ambassador on earth, then he must, by default, be the Pauline Antichrist, because – and this truth is held to be self-evident – no one but Christ can be Christ (I am referring to Luther's pamphlets *Adversus Execrabilis Antichristi Bullam*, and *De Antichristo*, both of which were translated into English as early as 1529).

But Nostradamus, who was born exactly 20 years after Luther, and died, once again, exactly 20 years after him – Luther's dates were 1483–1546, and Nostradamus's 1503–66 – read more into the New Testament concept of the Antichrist than even Luther did. Nostradamus believed that there were 'three' Antichrists, and that they were not necessarily super-human – that they could, in other words, come from amongst us, and not, via Satan and Express Delivery, direct from hell. It is 'human blood', after all, that 'reddens the water that covers the earth in hail' (*see* below), and not the bluer blood of fallen angels.

The following quatrain is the crucial one in Nostradamus's depiction of a trinity – rather than merely a solitaire – of Antichrists, and it repays close consideration. Please note, too, the mention of the number 'twenty-seven' in the quatrain which is, numerologically speaking, 3 times 9 – *ergo* the mirror image of 666, which biblical Revelations gives as the Number of the Beast (the mirror, in Kabbalism, reflected the dualistic aspects of God, the knowable and the unknowable, the revealed and the un-revealed, God and Satan, darkness and light – neither aspect of which is contradictory, as all aspects are incorporated within God's perfect unity).

The verse I'm referring to is Nostradamus's quatrain 8/77 (*see* the year 2077 in my section on the Third Antichrist for a commentary), and reads as follows:

> *L'antechrist trois bien tost annichilez,*
> *Vingt & sept ans sang durera sa guerre,*
> *Les heretiques mortz, captifs, exilez,*
> *Sang corps humain eau rogie gresler terre.*

The Third Antichrist will soon be annihilated
His war will have lasted for twenty-seven years
The heretics are either dead, captive, or exiled
Human blood reddens the water that covers the
earth in hail.

Sticking with our mirror imagery for a moment, the Antichrist's relationship to Satan is considered by many to be analogous to that between Christ and God. The very fact that Jesus Christ encapsulated 'perfect good' logically necessitated the creation of an antithesis, goes the argument. C G Jung, in his *Answer To Job* (from Volume 11 of the *Collected Works*) declared that the conditions for the creation of an Antichrist were present 'when God incarnates only in his light aspect and believes he is goodness itself, or at least wants to be regarded as such. An *enantiodromea* [change to the opposite] in the grand style is the coming of the Antichrist, which we owe more than anything else to the activity of 'the spirit of truth'.'

May we then assume that Nostradamus's concept of the 'third' Antichrist goes even further? Might it mirror the Holy Trinity, perhaps, possibly symbolized by the pope's triple crown or *triregnum*? (Please note that I am not referring here to the so-called Luciferian trinity, common to the Black Tradition, and which was said to consist of Samael, Lilith, and Cain).

Nostradamus was certainly obsessed by the number 3. Alongside the 'holy number' 7, which appears exactly 50 times within his 942 quatrains (*see* the third paragraph in my chapter on 'Nostradamus's Antichrists'), Pythagoras's 'perfect number' 3, symbolic of a beginning, a middle, and an end (and thus, by default, the Deity), takes equal precedence, with an intriguingly analogous total of 50. The following short riff on the number 'three' might possibly help to illustrate the number's larger symbolical significance.

To begin with, of course, men and women are, themselves, threefold, with the body, the soul, and the spirit. Their enemies, too, are threefold, consisting of the world, the flesh, and the devil – the Romans even carved the soul up into three further constituent parts, with the *manes*, the *anima* and the *umbra*. Situated well beneath the Holy Trinity in the pecking order, there were traditionally three estates of the realm in the Christian world, encapsulated by the nobility, the clergy, and the commonality, and furthermore the laws which governed the populace, at least in England, were subject to three tests (as they still are to this day), via the Commons, the Lords, and the Crown. The Classical world, too, was considered to be under the control of three main gods, namely Jupiter, who controlled the heavens, Neptune, who controlled the sea, and Pluto, who controlled the underworld, with the Jupiter/Jove entity symbolized by three-forked lightning, the Neptunian entity by a three-forked trident, and the Plutonian entity by a three-headed dog.

In addition there were three Classical Furies, three Graces, three Harpies, and three Sibylline Books. Three Nymphs guarded the fountain of Hylas, three more Nymphs (the Thriae) guarded Mount Parnassus, and there were three-times-three Muses, whilst the pythoness at Delphi sat, needless to say, on a tripod. There were three Chinese sovereigns or creator-Gods, named Fu-hsi, Shen Nung, and Yen-ti, as well as three Taoist celestial immortals, known as the Pure Ones, in the form of Lao-tzu, Tao Chun, and Yü Huang, mirrored by three Animal Poisons in the wheel of law – a bird, a pig, and a snake – together with Three Great Men, Three Great Beings, and Three Door Gods, just as in Buddhism there are Three Bodies Doctrine – *nirmana-kaya*, *sambhoga-kaya*, and *Dharma-kaya*.

Even the Christian Graces are threefold, in Faith, Hope, and Charity, as are the three kingdoms of Nature (animal, vegetable and mineral). There are three books of the Bible, consisting of the Old Testament, the New Testament, and the Apocrypha. There are three capital colours, red, yellow and blue, and the three wise kings, Melchior, Gaspar, and Balthazar, visited the infant Jesus in the stable, and they were called the Magi, with the word itself needing to be taken, according to Camoëns's *Lusiad*, to mean the same as the Indian word Brahmin. As we know that Brahma was one of the three beings created by God to 'assist' in the creation of the world, the whole charivari neatly goes to prove the potential interconnectedness of nearly every myth, dogma, and theocracy under the sun.

But Nostradamus wasn't alone in predicting multifarious Antichrists. Alexander Leighton, in his *Speculum Belli Sacri* (Amsterdam 1624) seems to be implying something similar with his 'The fourth ground of your hope is from the enemy with whom you have to deal, namely the Beast, the Dragon and the false Prophet, whose ruin the Lord of Hosts hath vowed and determined. It is a great advantage to know our enemies, but a greater encouragement to know that our enemies are God's enemies.'

The Beast. The Dragon. The False Prophet. Could the 'Beast' be the mirror image of the Father, the 'false Prophet' that of the Son, and the 'Dragon' that of the Holy Ghost?

The New Testament concept of the Antichrist as more than one single entity originated in 1 John (The First Epistle General) 2:18: 'Little children, it is the last time: and as ye have heard that antichrist shall come, even now are there many antichrists; whereby we know that it is the last time.' (Literal translation from the Greek: 'Little boys, it is the final hour, and just as you have heard that the antichrist is coming, now there are many antichrists; from which we may deduce that the last hour is here.')

Four verses on, John becomes even more specific about the Antichrist's makeup: 'Who is a liar but he that denieth that Jesus is Christ? He is antichrist, that denieth the Father and Son.' (Literal translation from the Greek: 'Who is the liar if not the one denying that Jesus is not Christ; this one is the antichrist, the one denying the Father and the Son.')

In chapter 4: verse 3 John makes his case even clearer: 'And every spirit that confesseth not that Jesus Christ is come in the flesh is not of god: and this is that *spirit* of antichrist, whereof ye have heard that it should come; and even now already is it in the world.' (Literal translation from the Greek: 'Every spirit which is confessing Jesus Christ in flesh having come out of the God it is, and every spirit which is not confessing that Jesus is out of the God is not; and this is the spirit of the antichrist which you have heard is coming, and which is now in the world already.')

John's final say on the matter comes in 2 John 7: 'For many deceivers are entered into the world, who confess not that Jesus Christ is come in the flesh. This is a deceiver and an antichrist.' (Literal translation from the Greek: 'Because many errant ones went out into the world, the ones not confessing Jesus Christ coming in the flesh; such is the errant one and the antichrist.')

So what we are left with is an image of one who is primarily a 'deceiver'. A being who pretends to be what he is not. A being who puts himself forward in the guise of another, greater being. 'The crooked Serpent creeps upon the earth, / An antichristian presbyter by birth.' (From the anonymous single sheet *The Watchman's Warning-Peece. Or, Parliament Souldiers Prediction*)

The British Library, to take but one example, has somewhere in the region of 780 books with the word 'Antichrist' in the title. Most of them are 19th-century sermons excoriating the pope for allegedly putting himself in Jesus Christ's place. They usually have titles like John Henry Hopkins's *A Candid Examination of the Question Whether the Pope of Rome is the Great Antichrist Of Scripture* (New York 1868), or Hugh McNeile's *The Church of Rome Proved to have the Marks of Antichrist* (London, The Protestant Association, 1843). Some are even more explicit, like Leonell Sharpe's *A Looking-*

Glasse for the Pope. Wherein he may see his owne face, the expresse image of Antichrist. Together with the Popes new creede, containing 12. articles of superstition and treason, set out by Pius the 4. and Paul the 5. masked with the name of Catholike faith: refuted in two dialogues (London 1616). Even good old Ramon Llull, the Mallorcan mystic and troglodyte, got into the act with his *Llibre dels articles de la fe : Llibre què deu hom creure de Déu; Llibre contra Anticrist*, presumably, given Llull's dates of 1232–1316, written towards the turn of the 14th century (and republished in Palma in 1996, by the Patronat Ramon Llull). Martin Luther, needless to say, defined his own take on the matter in 1523, in his *Offenbarung des Andtckrists; or, Antichrist revealed. Translated from the original high German.... By ... C. Smyth. ... Wider Catharinum, Wittenberg, M.D.XXIIII* (London 1846). But William Langland's *Piers Plowman* (written circa 1360-87) also mentions him, as does the Northumbrian 'Middle English' *Cursor Mundi* (written circa 1300).

Many of the books are written in German, French, or Dutch, alongside the more usual British and American editions. Some attempt to refute Protestant accusations – others attack the Quakers. Some are Protestant attacks on other, different sorts of Protestants. King Charles I, for instance, called Oliver Cromwell an 'Antichrist' – the feeling was, unsurprisingly, reciprocated – despite the fact that Cromwell's tutor, Thomas Beard, could say in the preface to his *Antichrist the Pope of Rome* (London 1625) that 'next to our Lord and Saviour Jesus Christ, there is nothing so necessary as the true and solid knowledge of Antichrist'.

Speed was of the essence when it came to hurling brickbats, apparently. Sink your blade in before the other man, because all – even the illiterate – understood the coterminous implication. Once tarred with the Antichristian brush, everybody knew that the story would run and run, not least because poets like Phineas Fletcher, Edmund Spenser, George Herbert, John Milton, George Wither, William Alabaster, and John Donne were only too happy to further disseminate the notion in their verse.

The Antichrist was a subject of intense fascination even to the most learned men of the times, including, it has to be said, the great Sir Isaac Newton, discoverer of gravity, and John Napier, the inventor of logarithms – even King James VI of Scotland (the 'wisest fool in Christendom' *pace* Sir Anthony Weldon) published a pamphlet on the subject a full 15 years before succeeding to the Crown of England as King James I.

Samuel Pepys – always one to live dangerously – admitted that he had enjoyed reading Francis Potter's claimed solution to the riddle of the biblical number 666 in *The Key Of The Revelation* (London, 1643), which attempted to prove, via mathematical deduction – and once and for all (or so Potter averred) – that the pope was indeed the Antichrist. And this in his diary entry dated 18 February 1666!

Books about the Antichrist mostly span the period from the 16th century to the early 20th century, when they somewhat peter out. There is much mention of 'calumnies', 'end-Christs', and 'true and false temples'. Some even dispute the number of the beast. Richard Franklin, in a pamphlet published in London in 1685, states that it should not be 666 but rather 42, and that Mahomet is actually the Antichrist, and that Christians should, in consequence, be let off the hook. So-called heretics and schismatics – which included Cathars, Albigensians, Waldensians, Arminianists, Spiritual Franciscans, Lutherans, Calvinists, Huguenots, Lollards, Czech Brethren, Hussites, Taborites, etc. etc. etc. – also found the Antichrist a useful weapon to launch at whichever version of the Mother Church they happened to be disagreeing with at that exact moment. It was duly launched back at them.

In France, the formerly Protestant King Henri IV was deemed to have defected to Antichrist in the year 1593, when he made his pragmatic decision that '*Paris vaut bien une messe*' ('Paris is surely worth a mass') – words that, according to the Catholic League, constituted his spiritual rebirth, finally entitling him to the throne of France (*see* 4/93 – 1593: The Expedient Conversion of Good King Henri of Navarre, in my *The Complete Prophecies Of Nostradamus*). This did not prevent him from being assassinated 17 years later, in 1610, by a disenchanted Catholic zealot still angered by Henri's continued tolerance towards the Huguenots, as manifested in the religiously enlightened 1598 Edict of Nantes. Cardinal Richelieu's later defeats of the Huguenots under Henri's son, Louis XIII, did nothing to soften the Antichristian backlash.

We may deduce, therefore, that the word Antichrist rapidly became a convenient stick with which to beat just about anybody who disagreed with you. It remains so to this day.

One thing we do know for certain, though, is that they were all wrong.

The Antichrist (or, according to Nostradamus, the third and final Antichrist) has not come upon us yet. A certain H W Antichrist did indeed write *A Letter of Condolence and Congratulation from Antichrist to John Bull; and the answer* (London 1795), but I think we may safely discount him as a contender for the main man.

The first thing to remember is that the Antichrist is not necessarily always known as the Antichrist. He is occasionally known as the Man of Sin – *see* William Hughes's *The Man of Sin: or a Discourse of Popery, wherein the ... Abominations ... of the Romish Church are ... exposed so to open light that the very blind may see them, and Antichrist in capital letters engraven on them: particularly in the infinite drove of ... Lying Wonders and Miracles. By no Roman, but a reformed Catholick* (London 1677), or Henry Denne's *The Man of Sin discovered: whom the Lord shall destroy with the brightnesse of his coming, etc* (London 1645). Hughes was actually a Hospitaller of St Thomas's, Southwark, so he may have had something of a vested interest in keeping his patrons sweet, and Denne was a Protestant Divine, so he had no conceivable choice in the matter.

The dramatist Ben Jonson (whose *Bartholomew Fair* I quote in my epigraph) clearly enjoyed satirizing such men as these. His anally-retentive Puritan, Ananias, in Act iv Scene vii of *The Alchemist*, even goes so far as to greet a man clothed in the split-sleeved Spanish fashion – go and look at Frans Hals's 1624 painting of the *Laughing Cavalier* in London's Wallace Collection for a fair approximation of what he is talking about – with the words: 'Thou look'st like Antichrist, in that lewd hat!'

The 'Man of Sin' cognomen stemmed from John Calvin and the Geneva translation of the Bible, of course, and, more to the point, to the notes pertaining to it – notes with which both Denne and Hughes would have been achingly familiar (*see* the third paragraph, line 16, of the Dedication to King James of the Authorized Version of the Bible, for a clever reiteration). Other expedient nicknames include the Wilful King, the Devil's Vicar, the God of Blood, the Son of Perdition, the Adversary, the Dragon, the Beast (*see* my epigraph again), the Whore of Babylon, the Little Horn, the Mystery of Iniquity, Lateinos or the 'Latin Man', and the False Prophet.

This scattergun approach to nomenclature takes us neatly to Nostradamus's own concept of the Antichrist, which is a far cry indeed from that of Luther and the Protestant Church; for the French version of the Antichrist is the *Antéchrist*, with the obvious implication that the Beast will be someone who comes 'before' (*anté-*) the End of Days. The English understanding of anti- always tended more to the strictly Latinate sense of the word, meaning not merely 'opposed to' but also 'equivalent to' or acting as a 'substitute for'. Such verbal differentiation is crucial, as we shall see.

NOSTRADAMUS'S ANTICHRISTS

I spent pretty much seven days a week for a full year writing my *The Complete Prophecies of Nostradamus* (Watkins 2009), and it gradually became clear to me during that extended period of work that Nostradamus had dedicated a really lengthy series of personalized quatrains to only three main historical figures – the first was Napoleon Bonaparte (47 quatrains), the second was Adolf Hitler (30 quatrains), and the third was someone whom we may term the 'One Still To Come' (36 quatrains).

Why should this be? The answer seems to lie in what Nostradamus believed. Namely that the world of men would abide for only 7,000 years – give or take the extra span of a man's life – from the birth of Jesus Christ. His final prophecy, quatrain number 10/74 – 7074, is categorical on the subject (*see* the end of my chapter entitled 'The Third Antichrist: 'The One Still To Come' for the full commentary):

Au revolu du grand nombre septiesme
Apparoistra au temps ieux d'Hacatombe,
Non esloigné du grand eage milliesme,
Que les entres sortiront de leur tombe.

When the great number seven completes itself
Games will begin at the Tomb side
Not far from the turn of the Millennium
The dead will rise out of their graves.

Nostradamus is not alone, of course, in imbruing the number 7 with exceptional significance, for 7 has long been considered a holy number. The moon, for instance, has seven phases, just as there are seven bodies in alchemy, seven senses, seven deadly sins, seven virtues, and seven spirits before the throne of God. There were seven days in creation, seven graces, seven days needed for Levitical purification, seven days in the week, seven wise masters, and seven great champions of Christendom. There are seven divisions in the Lord's Prayer, seven ages in the life of man, seven 'falls' each day by the just, each seventh year is deemed sabbatical, and seven-times-seven years is taken to represent a jubilee. Seven weeks demarcated the first two of the great three Jewish feasts, each of which lasted for seven days, just as there are seven churches of Asia, seven candlesticks, seven trumpets, seven stars, seven horns, seven eyes attributed to the Lamb of God, ten-times-seven Israelites on the move to Egypt, who were then exiled for seven years, and who lived under the nominal guidance of ten-times-seven elders. There are, in addition, seven bibles or sacred books (the Christian Bible, the Scandinavian Eddas, the Five Kings of the Chinese, the

Mohammedan Koran, the Buddhist Tri Pitikes, the three Vedas of the Hindus, and the Persian Zend-Avesta), seven joys and seven sorrows of the Virgin, seven chakras in Hindu kundalini, seven brothers of the Mayan Father Sun and seven Mayan corporeal power centres, seven sages of Greece, and even, dare one say it, seven wonders of the ancient world.

The three Antichrists which Nostradamus delineates are all contained within a period of 700 years from Nostradamus's birth, however, leading us to believe that the seer felt that he was only able to see that far into the future. Does this mean that there are more Antichrists to come? If so, Nostradamus does not address them.

What, then, unites the three disparate figures Nostradamus chooses as his Antichrists? What characteristics do they share in common? I think it might be a nice Sherlock Holmesian exercise to identify the principal aspects of the first two on his list, and in this way to predict, with a fair degree of accuracy – and pretty much by default – the character of the 'One Still To Come'.

First and foremost on Nostradamus's list was Napoleon Bonaparte, who was a born Catholic. True, he lapsed somewhat during his lifetime, using religion as an expedient tool with which to influence and manipulate people, even claiming that 'religion is what keeps the poor from murdering the rich'. But Napoleon was also able to confide to his friend, Charles Tristan, marquis de Montholon, towards the end of his life on St Helena (one may assume that conditions had not been so very bad on Napoleon's journey into exile, for de Montholon's wife, Albine, had shared her favours evenly between her husband and Napoleon, such that her subsequent, though non-legitimized daughter, Hélène Napoleone Bonaparte, could have belonged to either one of them):

> Alexander, Caesar, Charlemagne and I myself have founded great empires; but upon what did these creations of our genius depend? Upon force. Jesus alone founded His empire upon love, and to this very day millions will die for Him... When I saw men and spoke to them, I lighted up the flame of self-devotion in their hearts... Christ alone has succeeded in so raising the mind of man toward the unseen, that it becomes insensible to the barriers of time and space.

This sounds perilously close to an affirmation by Napoleon that he had, indeed, been fundamentally Antichristian in his megalomaniacal drive, and that he regretted this, and, in particular, the emotional manipulation of others via his own quasi-iconic status. Only his use of the word 'genius' in the first line might serve to suggest – to the very sceptical – a certain measure of recidivism.

Second in line is Adolf Hitler, a born Catholic who believed that Jews were the killers of God, and whose religion was summed up in the words: 'We do not want any other god than Germany itself. It is essential to have fanatical faith and hope and love in and for Germany.' Hitler, too, was a megalomaniac, and also took great pleasure in the emotional manipulation of others via a skilfully crafted quasi-iconic status. In the case of Hitler, however, there was no belated deathbed recantation (even if half-hearted), nor any sudden conversion back to Christian values.

There are other differences, too. Napoleon, as far as we know, did not consciously indulge in genocide – although he was responsible for the death, both directly and indirectly, of more than 3,000,000 people – whilst Hitler did. Thus, in the case of Nostradamus's first two Antichrists, we are faced with a steady increment in Antichristian power – hegemony, vainglory, and brutality in the first instance, followed by tyranny, vainglory, and mass murder in the second, but this time with a more than tenfold increase in the number of victims.

This brings us to the third in Nostradamus's diabolical trio – the 'One Still To Come'. The one he describes in quatrain 10/10 – 2010: Advance Warning of Third Antichrist, as 'Stained with mass murder and adultery / This great enemy of humanity / Will be worse than any man before him / In steel, fire, water, bloody and monstrous.'

All three Antichrists are 'tempters'. They work by 'signs and wonders'. They are quasi-superhuman, and are treated, by certain of their adherents, as virtual gods. They are pseudo-Messianic. They attract former true believers to a transformed, and thus flawed, new model of faith. They are perverters of men. They inhabit false doctrine as if born to such chameleonic cloth. They are 'workers of wonders', à la Belial (a.k.a. Beliar, a demon in the Bible who characterizes wickedness and worthlessness) and Simon Magus (a.k.a. Simon the Sorcerer, 'the source of all heresies', and a 'demon in human form'). They resemble the 'sleeping king/emperor' of the *Apocalypse of Pseudo-Methodius*, who will one day arise – like Barbarossa and King Arthur and countless other sleeping monarchs both before and after them – dragging vast armies in their wake, with which they will attempt to reconquer the lost world of heretofore.

A close reading of Nostradamus would also suggest that the Third Antichrist will once again be a Christian (Roman Catholic, Greek Orthodox or Russian Orthodox one presumes) if he is born – as Nostradamus would appear to be positing in his quatrain 2/32 – 2032: Birth of the Third Antichrist – Presage II – in either Italy, Croatia, Romania, Serbia, or Slovenia. This would tie in with the long-held belief that only an anti-Christian can be an Antichrist, and negates any half-baked ideas that the Antichrist will be a Muslim, a Hindu, a Jew, or a Buddhist. For the essence of Antichrist, as we have learned from Daniel xi. 36 & 2 Thessalonians ii. 4, will be 'enmity to God', and not adherence to a parallel, and possibly competitive, faith. A Christian who then becomes an atheist whilst still maintaining his Christian disguise for purposes of political expedience would appear to fit the bill perfectly, therefore, and nicely widens the neck of our net.

We are then left with the thorny question of whether the Third Antichrist's main impact will be primarily focused on the Christian world and on Christian belief. In that case the recent move away from organized religion might be viewed, in some quarters at least, as Antichristian in essence, leading to decadence, lawlessness, and the re-energizing of the Devil.

Insofar as Nostradamus believed that the past and the future were always concatenated in the present, he would appear to be suggesting something along similar lines in his next to last 'Great Comedian' quatrain, which I will précis here, and which T S Eliot was probably thinking of when he wrote the opening lines of Burnt Norton (Number 1 in the Four Quartets):

Time present and time past
Are both perhaps present in time future,
And time future contained in time past.
If all time is eternally present,
All time is unredeemable.

A pretty neat encapsulation, if you like, of the 'One Still To Come', a.k.a. he 'that was, and is not, and yet is' according to the Apocalypse of John (xiii, xvii).

The Great Comedian

Date: 7073
Nostradamus's Index Date: 73
Century Number: 10

Le temps present avecques le passé
Sera iugé par grand Iovialiste,
Le monde tard lui sera lasse,
Et desloial par le clergé iuriste.

Time present and time past
Will be judged by the great comedian
The world will tire of him when it is too late
Having forsaken its conventional clergy.

PART ONE

THE FIRST ANTICHRIST: NAPOLEON BONAPARTE

After a brief lapse, there was a rather curious revival of interest in the Antichrist in France during the period of the Enlightenment (a period dating from roughly the middle of the 17th century to the beginning of the French Revolution in 1789).

This revival reached fever pitch during the Revolution itself, with tracts and fomentations galore, often echoing and reiterating earlier tracts which predicted the fatal weakening of the Antichrist during the period 1794–1848. Some even predicted the arrival of the Second Beast as occurring in 1796, plum in the middle of the Revolutionary period. A 1796 English pamphlet, for instance, based partly on John Owen's 17th-century sermons and partly on Puritan theologian Thomas Goodwin's *Exposition of the Revelation* – the pamphlet was called *The French Revolution Foreseen in 1649* – imagined the coming Antichrist as specifically targeting papal power, which proved to be a pretty fair guess, in the circumstances, as Napoleon Bonaparte was personally responsible for the downfall of at least two popes.

This theory was further reinforced by a pamphlet of 1795 categorically entitled *Antichrist in the French Convention*, which was predicated on a similar series of occurrences. As we can see from Nostradamus's Napoleonic Timeline, and from the anti-papal Napoleonic quatrains which follow, this ties in very neatly with Nostradamus's 'Bonaparte as the First Antichrist' theory, and predates Napoleon's actual papal adventures by a fair number of years.

NAPOLEON BONAPARTE'S BIRTH CHART

Born: Tuesday 15 August 1769

Time: 11.34 (LMT -0.09)

Place: Ajaccio, Corsica, France

Location: 41N55 8E44

Planetary Placements

Sun in Leo

Ascendant in Scorpio

Moon in Capricorn

Mercury in Leo

Venus in Cancer

Mars in Virgo

Jupiter in Scorpio

Saturn in Cancer

Uranus in Taurus

Neptune in Virgo

Pluto in Capricorn

Midheaven in Leo

North Node in Sagittarius

Planetary Aspects

Sun: Square challenging Jupiter

Sun: Conjunct uniting with Midheaven

Moon: Opposition confronting Mercury

Moon: Opposition confronting Saturn

Mercury: Square challenging Uranus

Mercury: Square challenging Ascendant

Venus: Trine harmonizing Jupiter

Venus: Sextile cooperating with Neptune

Venus: Opposition confronting Pluto

Venus: Trine harmonizing with Ascendant

Mars: Sextile cooperating with Jupiter

Mars: Trine harmonizing with Uranus

Mars: Conjunct uniting with Neptune

Mars: Trine harmonizing with Pluto

Mars: Sextile cooperating with Ascendant

Jupiter: Opposition confronting Uranus

Jupiter: Sextile cooperating with Pluto

Jupiter: Conjunct uniting with Ascendant

Uranus: Trine harmonizing with Neptune

Uranus: Trine harmonizing with Pluto

Uranus: Opposition confronting Ascendant

Neptune: Trine harmonizing with Pluto

Neptune: Sextile cooperating with Ascendant

Pluto: Sextile cooperating with Ascendant

Astrological & Numerological Summary

According to the Chinese zodiac Napoleon Bonaparte was born under the sign of the Ox (just as Adolf Hitler was). His element was the earth (just as Adolf Hitler's was). The Ox, or Water Buffalo, is a beast of burden, but also aggressive when roused. This year tends to produce born leaders with dogged, unbending natures, who are prepared to take extreme measures in order to retain power – Richard Nixon, for instance, is another key example of an Ox personality. Such people do not tend to take prisoners, and will not tolerate criticism. The surface nature of the Ox can appear gentle and outgoing, making them attractive and influential – a virtual necessity in the run-up to power. But this calm exterior may mask an easily aroused and stubborn temper, capable of carrying all before it. Such people are often fixed in opinion, and unswerving in view – as a counter to this, they may also be highly astute in terms of meticulous planning.

Leos, too, are born leaders, and often have magnetic personalities. They do not take criticism easily, and can retreat into their shells when they encounter setbacks. When Leo is twinned with a Scorpio ascendant however, as is the case with Napoleon, a lot of the best and most positive aspects of the Leo birth sign can be obviated by the Scorpio's passion for secrecy, intrigue, and drama on an industrial scale. Such personalities often reap the whirlwind later in life, when what they fear most comes to pass (one hardly dares mention Waterloo). These types definitely have the common touch, but they also have more than their fair share of vainglory. Napoleon's moon in Capricorn, too, shows us a cold, self-controlled nature, aloof, and superior by default – this is the classic background of the megalomaniac (Hitler, too, has his moon in Capricorn).

Numerologically, Napoleon Bonaparte's name adds up to 4 under Cagliostro's kabbalistic system, which is, in turn, based on that of Cornelius Agrippa, who based his theories on the Hebrew alphabet: N is 5, A is 1, P is 8, O is 7, L is 3, E is 5, O is 7, N is 5, B is 2, O is 7, N is 5, A is 1, P is 8, A is 1, R is 2, T is 4, and E is 5, making 76, i.e. 7 + 6 which equals 13, i.e. 1 + 3 which equals 4. Four, in this case, is Pythagoras's perfect square, which suggests endurance, firmness, and concentration of purpose – when seen in a purely negative aspect, these traits can lead to obstinacy and self-destruction. Four is also the 'earth' number – remember Napoleon's Chinese element was also earth – which can suggest an even surface, masking torments and disruptions (volcanoes, earthquakes) within.

NOSTRADAMUS'S FIRST ANTICHRIST/NAPOLEONIC TIMELINE

1793: The recapture of Marseille, which culminates in Napoleon's triumph and wounding at the siege of Toulon.

The French Republic declares war on Britain. As a result, in the December of that same year, Napoleon Bonaparte first emerges as a force to be reckoned with.

1796: Napoleon's Lombardy campaign of 1795–6 ends the 300-year-old Duchy of Milan.

Napoleon's conquest of Lombardy

1797: The Battle of Cape St Vincent scuppers Napoleon's plans for an invasion of the British mainland.

Napoleon overthrows the Directory, which incorporates the Council of the Five Hundred, in the coup d'état of 18 Brumaire.

Napoleon ends Pope Pius VI's temporal authority and takes him prisoner. The pope dies two years later.

Napoleon engineers the fall of the Venetian Republic.

1797–1809: Napoleon spreads his net around Europe.

1798: Napoleon Bonaparte's ancestry is investigated, together with his imprisoning of two popes.

The defeat at the Battle of the Nile scuppers Napoleon's Egyptian campaign.

1798–99: Napoleon triggers a series of wars, in response to King Ferdinand IV of Naples's doomed resistance.

1799: Admiral Sir Sidney Smith becomes Napoleon's bugbear.

Napoleon fails to take Acre.

Napoleon takes control of the French State in a successful coup d'état.

1800: The French Revolution ends and Napoleon takes over.

1800–9: Napoleon begins his conquest of Italy. It will take nine years.

1802: The Treaty of Amiens brings a short lull in the Napoleonic wars.

1802–14: Ravenna changes ownership and becomes part of Napoleon's Cisalpine Republic.

1803: Napoleon forces Ferdinand III out of Tuscany.

1804: Napoleon is consecrated Emperor of France. His doomed empire is compared to that of ancient Rome.

1805: Napoleon crowns himself emperor in Milan Cathedral.

Napoleon humbles Venice, turning her into little more than a tourist resort.

Nelson's victory at the Battle of Trafalgar destroys French naval power once and for all.

Napoleon annexes the Ligurian Republic of Genoa.

1807: Napoleon Bonaparte's future plans are predicted in this, his greatest ever year.

The Treaty of Tilsit draws the Russians and the Prussians onto Napoleon's side.

1808: Napoleon Bonaparte invades Spain, under the pretext of protecting the Spanish coast from the British.

Napoleon forces regime change in Spain, placing his own brother, Joseph, on the Spanish throne.

Spain, Portugal, and the United Kingdom unite
against Napoleon in the Spanish War of Independence.

Napoleon sets up the famous military school of
Prytanée National Militaire.

Napoleon Bonaparte is compared, unfavourably, to
Scipio Africanus.

1809: Cracks begin to show in Napoleon Bonaparte's
European fortress.

Napoleon annexes the Papal States and imprisons his
second pope.

Napoleon suffers his first ever land defeat at the Battle
of Aspern.

1810: Napoleon has turned most of Europe into his own
personal enclave.

1811: The Peninsular War starts to go against Napoleon.

The Duke of Wellington wins a crucial series of battles,
culminating in the Battle of Albuera.

1812: Napoleon seizes, and holds onto, Verona.

The Abbé de Foix and the Bonapartes find themselves
linked, thanks to the Peninsular War.

1813: Napoleon is defeated at the Battles of Vitoria and Leipzig, making this one of his worst ever years.

Jean-Baptiste Bernadotte, one of Napoleon's favourite marshals, cements his kingship of Sweden, and distances himself from his former master.

The Allies advance into France, threatening Napoleon on his own turf.

1816: The Duke of Wellington, Napoleon's nemesis, is investigated.

The Austrians regain the Kingdom of Lombardy-Venetia from the tired old hawk, Napoleon, following his exile.

1821: The death of Napoleon Bonaparte.

1840: Napoleon Bonaparte's body is disinterred in St Helena, and reburied at Les Invalides.

THE NAPOLEONIC
QUATRAINS

THE RECAPTURE OF MARSEILLE

1793

88
10

Piedz & cheval à la seconde veille

Feront entree vastient tour par la mer,

Dedans le poil entrera de Marseille,

Pleurs, crys, & sang onc nul temps si amer.

Foot and horse soldiers at the second watch

Will enter from the sea and devastate everything

They will enter Marseille stripped naked

Weeping, cries, blood and bitter times.

This quatrain depicts a seaborne attack in which the protagonists 'strip off' and swim ashore from their ships, accompanied by their 'horses'. It's an exciting picture, and it would not be the first time that Marseille had endured such an attack – one thinks of Trebonius's siege of Marseille in 49 BC, and that of Charles de Bourbon in 1524.

This is more likely to apply to the recapture of Marseille by the Campagnoles army of General Carteaux in 1793, however, and the appalling reprisals carried out by the revolutionary attackers once the city became theirs.

SUMMARY

The recapture of Marseille in 1793 from royalist forces, which culminated in the young Napoleon Bonaparte's triumph and wounding at the Siege of Toulon.

THE FRENCH REPUBLIC DECLARES WAR ON BRITAIN

DATE

1793

NOSTRADAMUS'S INDEX DATE

93

CENTURY NUMBER

I

Terre Italique pres des monts tremblera,

Lyon & coq non trop confederés,

En lieu de peur l'un l'autre s'aidera,

Seul Castulon & Celtes moderés.

Italian territory, near the mountains, trembles

Lion and cock are not well suited

In a fearful place one helps the other

Only the castle of Toulon and the Celts are moderated.

This appears to apply to the fourth year of the French Revolution (1789–99), when the French Republic saw fit to declare war against Britain, Spain, and the United Provinces (of which the Netherlands is now the successor state).

The 'lion' is England, therefore, and the 'cock', France. On 1 February 1793 France annexed what is now modern Belgium (but was then the Austrian Netherlands), and this triggered the formation of the First Coalition, which added Austria, Prussia and Sardinia ('Italian territory, near the mountains, trembles') to the anti-French stew.

The fourth line refers to the British Siege of Toulon (the 'castle of Toulon') in December of that same year, which saw the first emergence of Napoleon Bonaparte as a force to be reckoned with [see 10/88 – 1793: The Recapture of Marseille].

SUMMARY

A date-perfect and pinpoint-accurate quatrain about the fourth year of the French Revolution, with particular emphasis on the rivalry between England and France, precursor to almost 20 years of continuous warfare.

BEAUCAIRE & ARLES DURING THE SACKING OF LYON

1793

93
10

La barque neufve recevra les voyages,
Là & aupres transferont l'empire,
Beaucaire, Arles retiendront les hostages
Pres deux colomnes trouvees de porphire.

Voyages will be made in the new ship

The empire will be shipped here and there

Beaucaire and Arles will keep the hostages

Porphyry will be found near two columns.

'Porphyry' was the purple colour of 'empire' [see 1/43 – 1840: Napoleon Bonaparte's Disinterment], and 'porphyry columns' appear more than once in Nostradamus's verses (e.g. 9/32 – 1532: The Rape of Civilizations & the Conquest of Peru – see my *The Complete Prophecies of Nostradamus*). One wonders whether Nostradamus believed that one day, far in the future, this was the only way that great empires would be remembered?

Either way, the Provencal towns of Beaucaire/Urgenum and Arles/Arelate were mighty Roman centres (both are on the Rhone river and therefore amenable to shipping, being situated a mere 18 kilometres apart), and Nostradamus's index date of 93 guides us inexorably to October 1793, and to the fall and rape of Lyon after a two-month siege by Revolutionary Republican forces (the 'new ship' of state).

The 'hostages' are the bodies of the hundreds of Lyonnais victims of the siege and of its near-genocidal aftermath, many of whom must have floated down the Rhone past the two historic outposts, inadvertently serving as a stark reminder to both towns of what awaited their own citizens (both Arles and Beaucaire housed significant royalist movements).

Author's Note: While all this slaughter was going on, Napoleon was taking his first small steps towards creating a sparkling new French Empire by defeating the British at Toulon.

SUMMARY

A haunting quatrain, depicting the aftermath of the 1793 massacres at Lyon.

THE DUCHY OF MILAN

Le nouveau faict conduyra l'exercite,

Proche apamé iusques au pres du rivage,

Tendant secour de Milannoile eslite,

Duc yeux privé à Milan fer de cage.

The newly promoted one leads the army

He is nearly surprised close to the edge of the river

Help is offered by the Milanese elite

The Duke is deprived of his sight in Milan,
in an iron cage.

The word *'apamé'* is from *happâmes* (*happer*), meaning to be grabbed by something (like a crocodile, or a fish), or surprised by something when you are least expecting it. 'Milan' has been dominated in its time by the French, the Austrians, and the Spanish, and given the index date of 95, this quatrain probably refers to Napoleon's Lombardy campaign of 1795–96 ('the newly promoted one leads the army'), after which Milan was declared the capital of the Cisalpine Republic.

Milan, which had formerly been a duchy ('the Duke is deprived of his sight in Milan') and part of the Holy Roman Empire since 1395 (another echo of the index date), never reverted to that state, but instead became part of the Austrian-ruled Kingdom of Lombardy-Venetia after Napoleon's fall from grace in 1815.

SUMMARY

Napoleon's conquest of Lombardy in 1796 [*see* 4/90 – 1796] ended the 300-year history of the Duchy of Milan.

NAPOLEON'S CONQUEST OF LOMBARDY

DATE

1796

NOSTRADAMUS'S INDEX DATE

90

CENTURY NUMBER

4

Les deux copies aux murs ne pourront ioindre,

Dans cest instant trembler Milan, Ticin:

Faim, soif, doutance si fort les viendra poindre,

Chair, pain, ne vivres n'auront un seul bocin.

The two armies are not able to meet at the walls

In the instant of impact Milan and the Ticino tremble

Hunger, thirst, strong doubts will come to prick them

There will not be a mouthful of either flesh, bread, or provisions.

The word 'cest' in line two comes from the Latin *cæstus*, meaning to hit (it also describes the studded gauntlet used in Roman boxing). We are seeing a combat, therefore, between two great armies, close to Milan [*see* 9/95 – 1796: The Duchy of Milan] and the nearby Italian-speaking Ticino.

Nostradamus would appear to be six years out in his index dating here, as Napoleon conquered Lombardy in 1796, and immediately declared 'Milan' the capital of his Cisalpine Republic – he was later crowned there, in the Duomo.

SUMMARY

A close call, this, for Napoleon's conquest of Lombardy, with Nostradamus's index date of 90 only six years off the mark.

THE BATTLE OF CAPE ST VINCENT

14 FEBRUARY 1797

97

9

De mer copies en trois parts divisees,

A la seconde les vivres failleront,

Desesperez cherchant champs Helisees,

Premier en breche entrez victoire auront.

The naval force will be divided into three parts

The second wing will lack supplies

In desperation they will search for the Champs-Élysées

The first ones at the breach will have the victory.

The Elysian Fields (or in Hesiod's terms, the Isles of the Blessed) were traditionally situated on the outermost western reaches of the earth, where they were home to fallen heroes and virtuous warriors, who would live on to enjoy immortal bliss at the hands of the gods – in Nostradamus's time, however, the 'Champs-Élysées' consisted of fields and market gardens, providing homemade produce for the Parisian markets. Both of these clues, as we shall see, are of crucial importance in interpreting this quatrain, which has previously been wrongly ascribed to any number of other naval engagements, including Trafalgar.

The Portuguese Cabo de São Vicente (Cape of St Vincent) is at the extreme south-westernmost reach of Europe, and has been considered sacred to the gods since Neolithic times – in fact the Greeks and Romans knew it as the 'holy promontory', and it was taboo to spend even one night there, for fear of antagonizing the Oestriminis (serpent people), who called this land of the extreme west (or *Finis Terrae*) their home.

On 14 February 1797 (note the perfect correlation with Nostradamus's index date), the British and the Spanish fought a decisive naval engagement there, whose effect was to keep Napoleon's Spanish allies blockaded in their harbours for the next few years (until the 1802 Peace of Amiens) and to form an effective split between France and Spain, thereby frustrating Napoleon's long-term plan (which was dependent on Spanish naval aid) of invading Britain.

The Spanish fleet, had intended to join with the French fleet at Brest, to create an unstoppable force to counter the much smaller British Mediterranean fleet – an unexpected levanter (easterly wind) soon drove the Spanish fleet off course, however.

Sir John Jervis's British Mediterranean fleet took full advantage of this fact, and while the Spanish were vainly looking around for their French allies ('in desperation they will search for the Champs-Élysées'), Jervis, having received word of the Spanish fleet's whereabouts (but not its size) from Nelson, decided to attack – he was therefore horrified to discover, at the very last moment, that he was outnumbered two to one.

Nelson, scenting disaster, decided to disobey orders, and after Jervis's main fleet had effectively split the Spanish fleet in two ('the naval force will be divided into three parts'), he broke formation and pursued the larger, rather than the smaller, Spanish group. He was now in front of the Spanish, and a sitting duck. Jervis, to his credit, saw what Nelson was about, and cut his jib accordingly. Nelson's ship, the *Captain*, had as many as six Spanish ships firing down upon her at the worst moment in the battle, but at this point Nelson did an extraordinary thing – he got up close to the Spanish 80-gun *San Nicolás*, and boarded her. Then, using the almost unholy sense of initiative which was to stand him in such good stead eight years later, at Trafalgar, he crossed the *San Nicolás*'s deck with his men behind him, and boarded, via her, the 112-gun *San José*, which had become entangled with her rigging. This trick, of crossing one boat to board another, instantly became known as 'Nelson's patent bridge for boarding enemy vessels' by an admiring and grateful Royal Navy.

Summary

Nostradamus describes, to a tee, the crucial British victory at the Cabo de São Vicente, which constituted unmitigated good news for the British people, truncating, as it did, in one fell swoop, all Napoleon's plans for an invasion of the British mainland.

THE COUNCIL OF THE FIVE HUNDRED

1797

97

I

Ce que fer flamme n'a sceu paracheuer,

La doulce langue au conseil viendra faire.

Par repos, songe, le Roy sera refuer,

Plus l'ennemy en feu, sang militaire.

That which fire and flame could not complete

The soft tongue of the council chamber will contrive

Through sleep and dream the King will be denied

The more the enemy is on fire, military blood.

The keys here are the 'council' chamber and the 'denial' of the king, for the index date of 97 takes us to 1797, and the purging of royalists by the republicans in the Council of the Five Hundred (*Conseil des Cinq-Cents*), during the latter part of the French Revolution. Napoleon overthrew the Directory (which incorporated the Council) in the coup d'état of 18 Brumaire (the second month of the Republican calendar), two years later.

SUMMARY

A reference to the horrors of the revolution, and to the final overthrow of royalist elements in the Directoire in 1797.

POPE PIUS VI

Romain Pontife garde de t'approcher

De la cité qui deux fleuves arouse,

Ton sang viendras au pres de la cracher,

Toy & les tiens quand fleurira la rose.

Roman Pontiff, beware of approaching

The city washed by two rivers

You will spit blood neat that place

You and yours, when the rose blossoms.

This quatrain sounds almost tubercular, in the sense of 'spitting blood', together with the image of the 'rose blossoming' (a bloodstained handkerchief?).

The index date of 97 takes us straight to the meat of the matter, which involves the Jesuit Pope Pius VI and his nemesis, Napoleon Bonaparte. Napoleon's troops had invaded Italy in 1796, defeating the papal troops and occupying Ancona and Loreto. Pius was consequently forced to the treaty table at Tolentino, on 19 February 1797, but a riot blamed on papal forces later that same year opened the way for General Berthier's entry into Rome on 10 February 1798, which coincided with Napoleon's demand of an end to the pope's temporal authority.

The pope was then taken prisoner. He died six weeks after reaching Valence (which is indeed 'washed by two rivers', the Rhone and the Isère), on 29 August 1799.

SUMMARY

A triumphant, date-accurate quatrain depicting the Napoleon-fuelled downfall of Pope Pius VI.

THE FALL OF THE VENETIAN REPUBLIC

1797

Cela du reste de sang non espandu:

Venise quiert secours estre donné:

Apres avoir bien long temps attendu

Cité livrée au premier corn sonné.

What remains of the blood will not be spilled

Venice searches for help to be given

After a long wait

The city is handed over at the first bugle call.

The index date of 1 is four years out here, as the Venetian Republic lost its freedom – after 1,070 years of independent rule – to Napoleon Bonaparte, on 12 May 1797, when its lands were partitioned between France and Austria under the terms of the Treaty of Campo Formio.

SUMMARY

The 1797 Treaty of Campo Formio marked the end of the Republic of Venice, and the beginnings of Venice's long decline.

NAPOLEON SPREADS HIS NET AROUND EUROPE

Pau, Verone, Vicence, Sarragousse
De glaives loings terroirs de sang humides:
Peste si grande viendra à la grand gousse
Proche secours, & bien loing les remedes.

Pau, Verona, Vicenza, Zaragoza,

Swords from distant lands are warm with blood

So great a plague will come to the great shell

Help nearby, but remedies far off.

France, Italy and Spain – the geographical locations are certainly dispersed! The index date is the bugbear here, as the cities were really only linked during the Napoleonic Wars, with Wellington leaving a garrison at 'Pau', 'Vicenza' and 'Verona' coming under Napoleonic rule in 1797; and 'Zaragoza' being besieged two times by French armies in 1808 and 1809, culminating in the surrender of the city on 21 February 1809.

SUMMARY

This has to be about the Napoleonic Wars, although the index date is out by 20-odd years.

NAPOLEON BONAPARTE I

PAU, NAY, LORON plus feu qu'à sang sera.

Laude nager, fuir grand aux surrez.

Les agassas entree refusera.

Pampon, Durance les tiendra enferrez.

Pau, Nay, Loron, he will be more fire than blood

Swimming in praise, the great man hurries
towards the crossroads

He will deny entry to the magpies

Pampon and Durrance will keep confine them.

The obvious acronym 'Pau, Nay, Loron' in the first line stands for Napaulon Roy (Napoleon King – the Corsican-style spelling of Napoleon's Christian name is Napauleone, with the second part of the name referring to *leone*, a lion). The further suggestion that 'he will be more fire than blood' clearly refers to Napoleon's lineage and character, which was that of a soldier ('fire'), rather than that of the nobility ('blood'). In addition, Napoleon was born under a 'fire' sign, Leo (the lion – *see* above), which Nostradamus would have considered more than relevant. Napoleon also had Mars in Mars, or Mars in Virgo, depending on which astrological reading one adheres to, both of which go a long way towards explaining his warlike and practical nature. '*Agassa*' is the Provençal word for a magpie (or *pie*, in French), and the two *pies* are the two Piuses, both of whom were popes (Pius VI and Pius VII) whom Napoleon imprisoned and otherwise tormented during his reign, in 1798 (*see* index date) and 1809 respectively. Pius VI died barely a year after his forced deposition, whilst Pius VII lasted somewhat longer, despite spending more than half of his time as pope bickering with Napoleon, and demanding both the release of his 13 black cardinals (Napoleon had deprived them of various dignities, including their red robes), the return of the Papal States, and his own release from exile.

SUMMARY

An entirely successful quatrain, cleverly dissecting Napoleon Bonaparte's ancestry, and commenting on the essential character of the one man who, more than any other, haunts the political and emotional map of France, right down to dictating the very form the French State would take in the aftermath of his death.

THE BATTLE OF THE NILE

1798

98

I

Le chef qu'aura conduit peuple infini

Loing de son ciel, de meurs & langue estrange:

Cinq mil en Crete & Thessale fini,

Le chef fuiant sauvé en marine grange.

The chief who will have led the infinite people

Far from their own skies, towards strange customs
and languages

Five thousand are finished in Crete and Thessaly

The fleeing leader escapes in a grain ship.

The 'infinite people' was one of Nostradamus's favourite euphemisms for the French, and the index date of 98 takes us straight to Napoleon's 1798 Egyptian campaign ('far from their own skies, towards strange customs and languages'), and the run-up to the Battle of the Nile, which saw Napoleon, on his flagship *The Orient*, with 13 ships of the line, 4 frigates, and 280 subsidiary vessels, investing Crete on his way to Egypt ('Thessaly/Iannina', under Ali Pasha, had become an ally after the 1797 Treaty of Camp Formio). With the French army ashore, and the fleet anchored, Nelson took the initiative and ordered an immediate attack. Only 2 French ships of the line and 2 French frigates out of a total of 17 ships engaged managed to escape the ferocious British onslaught, but even these were later captured, leading to a total reversal of the Mediterranean status quo. The battle was a disaster for the French and a triumph for Admiral Nelson (despite the occupational hazard of yet another wounding – this time Nelson was struck over his already blinded right eye, causing a flap of skin to fall across his face, temporarily blinding him). Napoleon was in Egypt with his army when he heard the news that between 2,000 and '5,000' of his men had been either killed or wounded in a battle that was to prove in many ways the precursor for the Battle of Trafalgar – for the future Admiral de Villeneuve (later to command French forces at Trafalgar in 1805) was one of the few initial escapees from the battleground (though he was subsequently captured in Malta).

SUMMARY

A spot-on quatrain describing the run-up and aftermath to the 1798 Battle of the Nile.

NAPOLEON TRIGGERS
A SERIES OF WARS

1798–99

4

4

L'impotent prince faché, plaincts & querelles.
De rapts & pilles, par coqz & par libyques:
Grand est par terre, par mer infinies voiles,
Seule Italie sera chassant Celtiques.

The impotent prince is angry, groans and quarrels

Rapes and pillaging, by cocks and Libyans

The great one is landlocked, at sea an infinity
of sails

Only Italy drives away the French.

The 'cocks' are the French and the 'Libyans' the Ottomans – the index date may be six years out, but this is pretty clearly about the 1 August 1798 Battle of the Nile [*see* 1/98 – 1798: The Battle of the Nile], whose aftermath saw Napoleon's army landlocked in Egypt. 'Only Italy drives away the French' refers to King Ferdinand IV of Naples, who bravely declared war against France on 29 November that same year, and went on, with laudable optimism, to occupy Rome. France declared war on Naples on 4 December, and the Ottomans got into the act the following February by declaring war in their turn, following Napoleon's invasion of Syria.

SUMMARY

This quatrain makes clear reference to the events of 1798–9, when war was declared by all the parties appearing in the verse [*see* 9/99 – 1799: The Siege of Acre].

ADMIRAL
SIR SIDNEY SMITH

1799

85
6

La grand cité de Tharse par Gaulois

Sera destruite, captifz tous à Turban:

Secours par mer du grand Portugalois,

Premier d'esté le jour du sacre Urban.

The great city of Tarsus will be destroyed

By the French, and all those wearing turbans
captured

Help will come by sea, from the great
Portuguese one

The first day of summer will be the day of
Saint Urban.

'Saint Urban's day' is customarily held on 2 April, which makes it a little early for summer, but Pope Urban I was also made into a saint, and his feast day falls on 19 May, which is a little closer to home.

Urban was accounted a great converter of souls, and this is probably what Nostradamus is getting at in mentioning him at all, as Saint Paul the Apostle (a.k.a. Saul of Tarsus, and also a great converter) was born at 'Tarsus' (*see* line one), whose destruction drives the quatrain.

Napoleon certainly passed by Tarsus (which is in Turkey) during his 1799 Egyptian Campaign, but was finally driven back by the English, under Sir Sidney Smith, and the Turks, under Ahmed Jamzar Pasha [*see* 9/99 – 1799: The Siege of Acre].

SUMMARY

Napoleon once said of the Francophile Sir Sidney Smith: 'That man made me miss my destiny.' Nostradamus's reference to the 'great Portuguese one' also relates to Smith, who was given the Grand Cross Of The Tower And The Sword by the Portuguese Prince-Regent John, for saving the Portuguese royal family from the French in 1810.

THE SIEGE OF ACRE

1799

99

9

Vent Aquilon fera partir le siege,
Par murs geter cendres, chauls, & poussiere,
Par pluye apres qui leur fera bien piege,
Dernier secours encontre leur frontiere.

A wind from the north will cause the siege to
be lifted

They will throw ash, chalk, and dust from
the walls.

The rain which follows will make things
even worse

The last hope of help against their frontier.

The 1799 Siege of Acre [see index date and 6/85 – 1799: Admiral Sir Sidney Smith] marked the turning point in Napoleon's unsuccessful invasion of Egypt and Syria. The walled city was stoutly defended by Ottoman troops, with British forces, led by Commodore Sir Sidney Smith, offering pivotal artillery support. Acre was strategically crucial, in the sense that it straddled the route between Egypt and Syria, and its loss would have placed British India within Napoleon's grasp. Plague and harsh weather conditions ('the wind from the north' and 'the rain which follows') ensured that Napoleon's final assault on 10 May was a failure, causing the chastened leader to write: 'Had I been able to take Acre... I would have made myself Emperor of the East, and I would have returned to Paris by way of Constantinople.' The reference to 'they will throw ash, chalk, and dust from the walls' refers to an age-old siege tactic of throwing lime from the battlements, thus blinding the oncoming besiegers.

SUMMARY

This is clearly about the failed Siege of Acre, during which Napoleon's forces were battered and harried by the weather and by the plagues and fevers which ensued – unforeseen elements which were to cost him upwards of 2,000 men.

THE NAPOLEONIC COUP D'ÉTAT

19 NOVEMBER 1799

99

I

Le grand monarque que fera compaignie

Avec deux roys unis par amitié:

O quel souspir fera la grand mesnie:

Enfants Narbon à l'entour quel pitié!

The great monarch who will keep company

With two kings united by friendship

Oh how the great household will sigh

How piteous, children from around Narbonne!

This would appear to be Nostradamus's response to the long-term ramifications of Napoleon Bonaparte's 19 November 1799 coup d'état (*see* index date).

'Oh how the great household will sigh' seems an apposite description of the replacement of the Directoire by one-man rule, the arrogation of disparate European kingdoms by Napoleon's relatives and cronies ('two kings united by friendship' could describe a number of Napoleon's expedient royal placements), and the 16-year helter-skelter ride between peaks of glory and troughs of horror that Napoleon subsequently inflicted on the French people ('the children from around Narbonne').

SUMMARY

A prescient quatrain, describing the events following the 1799 coup d'état which gave Napoleon Bonaparte exclusive control of the French State.

THE END OF THE FRENCH REVOLUTION

Pour l'abondance de larme respandue

Du hault en bas par le bas au plus hault

Trop grande foy par ieu vie perdue,

De soif mourir par habondant deffault.

Thanks to the abundance of tears shed

By the high-born to the low-born, and vice versa

Too great a faith – a life lost in a game

To die of thirst through plentiful default.

There's a pretty paradox in the last line, as if the person concerned were dying of hunger in a granary – the rub is that he 'dies of thirst' despite the copious 'tears' everybody is shedding on each other's behalf.

It's an end-of-century quatrain, of course, and therefore general in intent, and most probably relates to 1800 and the aftermath of the French Revolution, in which the rights of man were at once both vindicated and travestied.

SUMMARY

A generalized quatrain depicting the ultimate failure of the French anti-monarchical 'game', which simply replaced one ineffectual tyrant with another, more effectual one, in the guise of Napoleon Bonaparte.

NAPOLEON'S CONQUEST OF ITALY

Le Duc voudra les siens exterminer,

Envoyera les plus forts lieux estranges,

Par tyrannie Pize & Luc ruiner,

Puis les Barbares sans vin feront vendanges.

The Duke will wish to exterminate his own people

He will send the strongest off to far-flung places

He will ruin Lucca and Pisa with his tyranny

Then the Barbarians will hold a grape harvest
without wine.

Napoleon invested both 'Lucca' (which had been an independent democracy/oligarchy for hundreds of years) and 'Pisa', during his conquest of Italy, placing both cities technically under the control of his son, Napoleon II, Duke of Reichstadt (who bore the somewhat vainglorious title King of Rome). Nostradamus seems to be suggesting here that Napoleon's tinkering with supranational borders opened up a can of worms, letting the 'Barbarians' in, just as happened during the decline and fall of the Roman Empire.

The index date of 80 presents us with certain further problems, as Lucca's downfall came in 1805, when it was handed over to Napoleon's sister, Elisa, Duchess of Lucca and Grand Duchess of Tuscany, along with Piombino (which 'Pisa' had traditionally ruled). The paralleling of Napoleon's often corrupt and venal siblings with the ancient Barbarians is, in some ways, a reasonable one, however, as both parties plundered and pillaged with impunity.

SUMMARY

Nostradamus compares Napoleon's conquest of Italy with that of the Barbarians during the decline of ancient Rome. His image of a 'grape harvest without wine' is an apposite one, and reflects the ravages Napoleon's family executed upon much of the Italian cultural heritage – a major part of which ended up either hopelessly disseminated or in the Louvre.

THE TREATY OF AMIENS

27 MARCH 1802

Par mort la France prendra voyage à faire

Classe par mer, marcher monts Pyrenées,

Hespagne en trouble, marcher gent militaire:

Des plus grands dames en France emmenées.

France has a journey to make because of death

The fleet at sea, and marching through the
Pyrenees

Spain in trouble, the army on the move

Great ladies brought to France.

The signing of the Treaty of Amiens on 27 March 1802 brought a short lull in the Napoleonic Wars. The main signatories were France, Britain, Spain, and the United Provinces, and a number of deals were made and agreements struck. In little more than a year, however, the war between Britain and France resumed its inevitable course, this time involving Spain as France's ally.

SUMMARY

A general quatrain dealing with the Treaty of Amiens and its immediate (and inevitable) aftermath. The signing of the treaty briefly opened France up once again to noble British tourists, with 'great ladies brought to France', including authors Maria Edgeworth and Fanny Burney.

RAVENNA CHANGES OWNERSHIP

La magna vaqua à Ravenne grand trouble,

Conduictz par quinze enserrez à Fornase

A Rome naistre deux monstres à teste double

Sang, feu, deluge, les plus grands à l'espase.

Magnavacca, near Ravenna, is in great trouble

Led by fifteen prisoners from Fornese

Two monsters with double heads will be born
in Rome

Blood, fire, flood, the greatest on the spars.

'Magnavacca' (meaning 'great cow' in Latin), was the name of a port near Ravenna, now known as Porto Garibaldi. '*Espase*', in line four presents a more formidable problem, however, as it could mean either a spar (*espars*), or a space (*espace*).

Nostradamus's index date of 3 comes to our rescue, however, for in 402 Ravenna was made the capital of the Western Roman Empire. This marked something of a high point in Ravenna's history until, 1,400 years later, in 1802, Ravenna found itself annexed by Napoleon's Cisalpine Republic, from which it transmogrified, in 1805, to the Kingdom of Italy, from whence it returned to the pope's care in 1814.

The 'monsters with double heads born in Rome' are therefore Napoleon (president and emperor) and Pope Pius VII (bishop of Rome and pope).

SUMMARY

This details the heady transmogrification of Ravenna during Napoleonic times from a member of the Cisalpine Republic, to a part of the Kingdom of Italy, to a member of the Papal States. Later, Ravenna, or a place with a similar name in Eastern Europe, was to become Nostradamus's putative birthplace for the Third Antichrist.

FERDINAND III

Le successeur de la Duché viendra.

Beaucoup plus oultre que la mer de Toscane,

Gauloise branche la Florence tiendra

Dans son giron d'accord nautique Rane.

The successor to the Duchy will come

Even further than the Tuscan Sea

A Gallic branch will hold Florence

In his lap lies a musty naval agreement.

The Grand 'Duchy' in question is that of Tuscany, which existed from 1569 to 1859. The 'Gallic branch' of the duchy came to power following the demise of the Medicis, in 1737, with the accession of Francis Stephen of Lorraine to the dukedom. Francis's grandson, Ferdinand III, was forced out of Tuscany by Napoleon, following the 1801 Treaty of Aranjuez, a move that began a heady series of geographical leaps for the young man, via Salzburg and Würzburg, culminating in his return to Tuscany in 1814, after Napoleon's first fall from power.

SUMMARY

The trials and travails of Ferdinand III, who was sent spinning from pillar to post by the Napoleonic Wars, until he ended up where he had begun – in Tuscany.

NAPOLEON'S DOOMED EMPIRE COMPARED TO THAT OF ANCIENT ROME

DATE

1804

NOSTRADAMUS'S INDEX DATE

4

CENTURY NUMBER

6

Le Celtiq fleuve changera de rivaige,

Plus ne tiendra la cité d'Agripine:

Tout transmué ormis le vieil langaige,

Saturne, Leo, Mars, Cancer en rapine.

The Celtic river will change its bank

It will no longer hold the Agrippan city

Everything transmuted except the old language

Saturn, Leo, Mars and Cancer are plundered.

'Rivers' don't 'change banks' or direction of flow, so we are talking in metaphor here, with 'Celtic', as usual, signifying French, and the 'Agrippan city' probably signifying Rome, which the great general, Marcus 'Agrippa' Vipsanius, embellished with the plunder from his victories at Actium and Philippi (the Pantheon, for instance, forms part of his great legacy). Nostradamus pulls us up short, however, by implying that there is little left of Agrippa's Rome now, save its 'old language'.

With all that duly taken on board, the index date of 4 leads us to that noted Agrippan impersonator, Napoleon Bonaparte, and his consecration as emperor, in Paris, by Roman Pope Pius VII, on 2 December 1804. Somewhat vaingloriously, Napoleon's son, Napoleon II, was known from birth as the King of Rome, and both he and his father are buried in Paris's very own pantheon, Les Invalides, with little else remaining of the empire they so assiduously craved.

SUMMARY

A quatrain comparing Napoleon Bonaparte's ambitions to those of Marcus Agrippa, and finding the former wanting. The quatrain anticipates Napoleon's comeuppance, and the long-term alchemical 'transmutation' of France which resulted (Saturn in Leo signifying personal alchemy, with Mars in Cancer implying acidity in the stomach, which, in the form of either arsenic poisoning or cancer, is what eventually killed Napoleon).

NAPOLEON IS CROWNED EMPEROR

26 MAY 1805

5

9

Tiers doit du pied au premier semblera.

A un nouveau monarque de bas hault

Qui Pyse & Lucques Tyran occupera

Du precedant corriger le deffault.

The third toe will resemble the first

Of a new monarch, raised from low to high

The tyrant will occupy Pisa and Lucca

And will correct the faults of his predecessor.

This can surely only apply to Napoleon Bonaparte, who crowned himself emperor in Milan Cathedral on 26 May 1805 (*see* index date), using the iron crown of the ancient kings of Lombardy. Nostradamus describes Napoleon to a tee, with the emphasis on his having risen from 'low to high' (Napoleon began as an artillery lieutenant and ended up as an emperor), and correctly points out that he 'tyrannized' Italy, ending 1,000 years of Venetian independence and partitioning the country between France and Austria in the 1797 Treaty of Campo Formio. Nostradamus would probably have considered the Emperor Nero to be Napoleon's tyrannical predecessor, and his comment about Napoleon 'correcting Nero's faults' may be taken as very much tongue-in-cheek – for it is, philosophically speaking, impossible for one tyrant to correct the faults of another for they are both, by definition, tyrants.

Summary

A brilliant, date-perfect quatrain, punning nicely on the 'toe' of Italy, and relating one tyrant (and owner of the toe) to another – Nero and Napoleon (both, it must be said, considered Antichristian by some).

NAPOLEON'S HUMBLING OF VENICE

26 DECEMBER 1805

6
4

D'habits nouveaux apres faicte la treuve,
Malice tramme & machination:
Premier mourra qui en fera la preuve
Couleur venise insidiation.

New clothes are put on after the truce

Malice, conspiracies, and machinations

The first to die is the one who proved himself

The Venetian colours are ambushed.

After the magnificence of its 18th century (the *settocento*), Venice was brought low by the machinations of Napoleon Bonaparte in the early part of the 19th century. It lost its independence after 1,070 years on 12 May 1797, and became Austrian territory 5 months later under the Treaty of Campo Formio. Napoleon snatched the city back ('the Venetian colours are ambushed') on 26 December 1805 (Nostradamus's index date of 6 is a bare six days out) under the Treaty of Pressburg, whereupon it became part of his Kingdom of Italy until 1814.

SUMMARY

Napoleon more or less destroyed Venice during the 17 years he was nominally in charge, turning it from a flourishing and refined centre of the liberal arts into little more than an occasional, and architecturally disintegrating, tourist resort. 'New clothes' indeed.

THE BATTLE OF TRAFALGAR

21 OCTOBER 1805

NOSTRADAMUS'S INDEX DATE
5
CENTURY NUMBER
4

Croix, paix, soubz un accompli divin verbe,
L'Hespaigne & Gaule seront unis ensemble.
Grand clade proche, & combat tresacerbe:
Coeur si hardi ne sera qui ne tremble.

The cross, peace, under one perfect divine word

Spain and France united

A great disaster is imminent, and very
bitter fighting

Even the hardiest heart will tremble.

Given the index date of 5 and the unlikely phrase 'Spain and France united', this quatrain must be about the 1805–7 War of the Grand Alliance (as opposed to the countless other wars of the Grand Alliance), which united a powerful France, under Napoleon Bonaparte, and a weak Spain, under Charles IV, against the Third Coalition of England, Portugal, Russia and Austria. On 21 October 1805, Admiral Horatio Nelson defeated the combined French and Spanish fleet at the Battle of Trafalgar, destroying French naval power once and for all. There is a wonderful pun for all English speakers in line four, with the word 'hardi', meaning 'hardy' – for Nelson was shot by a French sharpshooter during the battle, and his dying words to his Flag Captain, Sir Thomas Hardy, were: 'Kismet, Hardy.' (Others would have it that Nelson said 'Kiss me, Hardy', but that is unlikely, given the customs prevailing in the Royal Navy at that time).

SUMMARY

An incredibly accurate quatrain, date perfect, about the pivotal Battle of Trafalgar, and its effect on the unlikely union between France and Spain.

NAPOLEON'S ANNEXATION OF THE LIGURIAN REPUBLIC OF GENOA

1805

4

8

Dedans Monech le coq sera receu,

Le Cardinal de France apparoistra

Par Logarion Romain sera deceu

Foiblesse à l'aigle, & force au coq naistra.

The cock will be received inside Monaco

The French Cardinal will appear

The Roman Catholic will be deceived by Liguria

The eagle weakens, the cock strengthens.

Genoa is the capital of 'Liguria' (which borders 'Monaco'), and this quatrain, with its index date of 4, takes us directly to Napoleon Bonaparte, and his annexation of Genoa in 1805, which culminated in the formation of the Kingdom of Italy later that year.

Napoleon had been born in Corsica (which had become a Genoese dependency just a year before his birth), and, although technically Corsican, he was therefore Italian by ancestry. Genoa had originally been invaded by Napoleon in 1797, and the short-lived Ligurian Republic was annexed by France (the 'cock' is a French symbol, and the 'eagle' is the symbol of Savona, which belonged to Genoa) in 1805.

The reference to the 'Cardinal of France' in line two would appear to be a wicked one, referring to Pope Pius VII's consecration of Napoleon's grandiose crowning as emperor in Paris in 1804.

SUMMARY

A remarkably accurate quatrain – with all its symbols and place names intact – describing the fall of the Province of Genoa to the forces of Napoleon Bonaparte in 1805.

NAPOLEON BONAPARTE'S FUTURE PLANS PREDICTED

1807

7

10

Le grand conflit qu'on appreste à Nancy,

L'aemathien dira tout ie soubmetz,

L'isle Britanne par vin, sel en solcy,

Hem. mi deux Phi. long temps ne tiendra Metz.

The great battle being prepared at Nancy

The god of blood will say to all 'I will subjugate you'

The British Isles worried over wine and salt

Here! The one with half of two daughters won't hold Metz for long.

The last line has tormented commentators for centuries, but, given an old enough dictionary (Tarver's 1849 *Phraseological Dictionary*, for instance), it becomes very simple. '*Hem*' is an interjection for 'Here!' in Old French, '*mi deux*' means 'half of two', and '*Phi*' is an euphonic codeword for *filles* (daughters), the sound of which it mimics exactly.

And who had 'half of two daughters' (i.e. two illegitimate daughters)? Why, Napoleon Bonaparte, the 'god of blood' (*haema*/blood and *theos*/god), in the form of Hélène by the Countess Montholon (*see* my chapter entitled *Nostradamus's Antichrists*), and Emilie by Françoise-Marie LeRoy.

The year 1807 also saw the British fleet blockading French ports in an effort to prohibit the ships of neutral nations from trading with France ('the British Isles worried over wine and salt'), and both 'Nancy' and 'Metz' falling under Napoleon's aegis via the Treaty of Tilsit [*see* 6/7 – 1807].

Napoleon was to hold Metz for seven years ('won't hold Metz for long'), until his abdication in 1814.

SUMMARY

A fine quatrain detailing one of Napoleon's greatest ever years, 1807, and the response of the British to his projected plans for European domination.

THE TREATY OF TILSIT

Norneigre & Dace, & l'isle Britannique,

Pars les unis frères seront vexées:

Le chef Romain issue de sang Gallique,

Et les copies aux forestz repoulsées.

The snowy North, and Dacia, and the British Isles

Are troubled by the united brothers

The head of Italy has French blood

And the armies are repulsed from the forests.

This is a magnificent, date-perfect quatrain, describing the Treaty of Tilsit (1807) and its effects. The 'united brothers' mentioned in line two are, of course, those of Napoleon Bonaparte, whose sovereign rule was specifically recognized by this treaty between the French, the Russians (the 'snowy North') and the Prussians.

The treaty was signed on a raft on the Neman river, and effectively conceded to Napoleon all the land between the Rhine and the Elbe ('the armies repulsed from the forests'). The 'head of Italy who has French blood' was Joseph Bonaparte, King of Spain, Naples, and Sicily, with Louis Bonaparte being King of Holland, and Jérome, King of Westphalia – ergo 'the united brothers'.

SUMMARY

The 1807 Treaty of Tilsit, by which Napoleon agreed that Tsar Alexander I would act as his mediator in the negotiation of a separate peace with the 'British Isles'.

NAPOLEON BONAPARTE INVADES SPAIN

Les Cimbres ioints avecques leurs voisins,

Depopuler viendront presque l'Hespaigne:

Gents amassés Guienne & Limosins

Seront en ligue, & leur feront compaignie.

The Cimmerians unite with their cousins

They will depopulate almost all of Spain

People will congregate in Guienne and
the Limousin

They will act together, and keep them company.

The 'Cimbrians' were known to the ancient Greeks as the nomadic, horse-coping Cimmerians, natives of a region to the north of the Caucasus and the Black Sea, in what is now Russia and the Ukraine – the last historical record of them was in AD 515, so we may assume that Nostradamus is using them figuratively.

If it wasn't for the index date of 8, one would be tempted to go straight to the Spanish Civil War, and to Russia's intervention on the Republican side – ancient 'Guienne', too, covered a part of Aquitaine and Gascony that saw considerable Republican activity, with volunteers congregating there before transhipment over the border. Limoges, in the 'Limousin', was also a centre for Spanish loyalists (we know, for instance, that 26 were killed during the 1944 German massacre at Oradour-sur-Glane).

We are still left with the index date of 8, however. Might it take us instead to Napoleon's invasion of Spain with 70,000 troops in January 1808? After an 11-month to and fro, Napoleon returned with 150,000 men in the December of that year, triggering the 1808–14 Peninsular War.

SUMMARY

Napoleon Bonaparte used the guarding of the Spanish coast against the British as the pretext for his January 1808 invasion. Within five months he had placed his brother Joseph on the throne, triggering a popular uprising that was to transmogrify into the Spanish War of Independence.

REGIME CHANGE
IN SPAIN

Ceulx qui estoient en regne pour scavoir,

Au Royal change deviendront apouvris:

Uns exilés sans appuy, or n'avoir,

Lettrés & lettres ne seront à grand pris.

Those in the reign on account of their knowledge

Will be impoverished when the royal change happens

Some will be exiled without influence and without gold

Both learning and the learned will be accounted cheap.

Regime change in a year marked with an 8 takes us to 1808, and the ups and downs investing Spain. Napoleon Bonaparte, using the threat of British sea power as a pretext, occupied much of the country, forcing the abdication of, first King Charles IV, and then his son, Ferdinand VII.

In May Napoleon appointed his brother Joseph king of Spain, triggering the populist 2 May uprising (famously captured on canvas by Francisco Goya). Supporters of the previous regime were then either exiled or imprisoned, inadvertently hastening the 1808–14 Spanish War of Independence [*see* 1/8 – 1808].

SUMMARY

Napoleon tricked his way into Spain, and held the country in an iron grip from 1808 until 1814.

THE SPANISH WAR OF INDEPENDENCE

Combien de foys prinse cité solaire
Seras, changeant les loys barbares & vaines.
Ton mal s'approche: Plus seras tributaire
La grand Hadrie reourira tes veines.

How many times will the city of the sun be taken

It will be again, its laws changed in barbaric and unprofitable ways.

Your evil day approaches: You will not just be enslaved

Great Hadrian will reopen your veins.

The Puerta del Sol (Gate of 'the Sun') has been one of the central meeting places in Madrid for many hundreds of years. The Gate was originally part of the 15th-century city walls, and was named after the image of the rising sun that decorated the eastern-facing gate. Joachim Murat, the general in command of Napoleon's forces, entered the city by this gate on 26 March 1808, forcing the abdication of King Charles IV. Technically, Charles's eldest son, Ferdinand VII, became king in his place, but he, too, was forced to abdicate barely two months later by the French conquerors.

Napoleon Bonaparte then revealed his secret plan – to make his own brother, Joseph, king of Spain instead. This action triggered a popular revolt that led directly to the Peninsular War (a.k.a. the Spanish War of Independence 1808–14). The initial revolt was finally crushed by Marshal Murat at the cost of 150 French lives. Incensed, Murat then ordered large-scale reprisals, and the next day, 3 May, saw hundreds of Spanish citizens shot. Spanish painter Francisco Goya immortalized the scene on the Principio Pio Hill in his painting entitled *The Third Of May 1808* – an Antichristian image, if ever there was one.

One further Spanish connection manifests in the *Century* number: the Roman Emperor 'Hadrian' was born in Italica (close to Seville), a Roman colony in Spain, on 24 January, AD 76.

SUMMARY

The 'city of the sun' is Madrid, invaded and taken by Napoleon's French army in 1808. This action and its consequences directly triggered the Spanish War of Independence, in which Spain, Portugal and the United Kingdom successfully allied themselves against Napoleonic France.

PRYTANÉE NATIONAL MILITAIRE

Par le grand Prince l'imitrophe du Mans,

Preux & vaillant chef de grand exercite:

Par mer & terre de Gallotz & Normans,

Caspre passer Barcelone pillé isle.

By the great Prince bordering Le Mans

Brave and valiant leader of the large army

By land and sea French-speaking Bretons
and Normans

The goat will pass Barcelona and pillage
the island.

La Fleche is situated in the south of the Loire region of France, just 21 kilometres from 'Le Mans'. In 1808 Napoleon Bonaparte set up the Prytanée military academy there, transforming the original school, founded by Henri VI in 1604, into one of the six great military academies of France.

SUMMARY

A rather generalized quatrain, possibly relating to Napoleon's setting up of the Prytanée military academy near Le Mans.

NAPOLEON BONAPARTE & SCIPIO AFRICANUS

1808

8

8

Pres de linterne dans de tonnes fermez,

Chivaz fera pour l'aigle la menee,

L'esleu cassé luy ses gens enfermés,

Dedans Turin rapt espouse emmenee.

Near Linternum, locked inside some barrels

Chivasso will play dirty for the eagle

The elected one is exiled, his people imprisoned

His abducted wife is taken to Turin.

'*Linternum*' was in Campania, and the country home of Scipio Africanus, while 'Chivasso' is to the north of Italy, near Turin. Scipio, who felt under-appreciated by the Romans after his conquest of Hannibal, ordered that his bones should stay in Linternum, and he also famously refused to violate a princess brought to his tent after the fall of New Carthage, but instead sent her back to her parents, with wedding presents for her fiancé.

Nostradamus seems to be comparing these actions (well known to classically educated readers), with the behaviour of another conqueror, whom we may suppose, thanks to the index date of 8, to be Napoleon Bonaparte (Napoleon famously used the golden roman 'eagle' as the symbol of the new French Empire).

SUMMARY

Nostradamus compares Napoleon Bonaparte to Scipio Africanus, and finds him wanting.

NAPOLEON
BONAPARTE II

Neuf ans le regne le maigre en paix tiendra,

Puis il cherra en soif si sanguinaire:

Pour luy grand peuple sans foy & loy mourra

Tué par un beaucoup plus debonnaire.

The thin one will reign without let for nine years

Then he will fall in love with a thirst so bloody

That people with no laws and no faith will die
on his account

He will be killed by a kinder man.

This quatrain is about Napoleon Bonaparte (the little corporal), who reigned as emperor of France for a period of nine and three quarter years (he was crowned on 2 December 1804, and abdicated on 6 April 1814).

The year 1809 (*see* index date) saw both Wellington's victory at Talavera, and Napoleon's divorce from his first great love, Josephine de Beauharnais, who agreed to his remarriage on account of her inability to provide him with a son and heir. Three years later, Napoleon invaded Russia ('a people with no laws and no faith'), and his eventual downfall, leading to his death in 1821 on Saint Helena, was once again caused by the Duke of Wellington, this time at Waterloo, in 1815 – a 'kinder' and arguably more 'debonair' man than Napoleon altogether.

SUMMARY

A key year, 1809, for Napoleon Bonaparte, which saw not only his divorce from Josephine de Beauharnais, but also his first military defeat at the Battle of Aspern [*see* 9/9 – 1809: The Battle Of Aspern], closely followed by that of Talavera.

NAPOLEON ANNEXES THE PAPAL STATES

1809

9
6

Au sacres temples seront faicts escandales,

Comptés seront par honneurs & louanges:

D'un que on grave d'argent dor les medalles,

La fin sera en tourmens bien estranges.

Scandals will occur at the sacred temples

They will be accounted honourable and praiseworthy

Of one for whom medals in gold and silver are engraved

The end will manifest itself in very strange torments.

This quatrain is quite clearly about events surrounding Napoleon Bonaparte's 1809 annexation of the Papal States, and his subsequent imprisonment of Pope Pius VII. Napoleon (the 'one for whom medals in gold and silver are engraved') was to die 12 years later, in 1821, in agony from either cancer of the stomach or arsenic poisoning ('the end will manifest itself in very strange torments'). Nostradamus, who was a staunch Catholic, would probably have considered either as little more than his due, given his actions of 1809.

SUMMARY

Napoleon Bonaparte's 1809 annexation of the Papal States, and his five-year imprisonment of Pope Pius VII.

THE BATTLE OF ASPERN

1809

9

9

Quand lampe ardente de feu inextinguible

Sera trouvé au temple des Vestales,

Enfant trouvé feu, eau passant par crible:

Perir eau Nymes, Tholose cheoir les halles.

When the everlasting fire of the burning lamp

Is found in the Vestal temple

The child will burn, water passing through
the sieve

Nîmes perishes in water, the Toulouse markets
will fall.

The 'Vestal' virgin's job was to keep the sacred flame of the home-goddess Hestia alight – as long as this was done, Rome would prosper.

Nostradamus foresees a time when the French fires are doused by flood, with the flame turning on its keeper ('the child will burn'). The seeds for this were sown in 1809, at the Battle of Aspern, where Napoleon suffered his first ever military, as opposed to naval, defeat. Six years later he lost France.

SUMMARY

Nostradamus sees the writing on the wall, as France's vestal light begins to sputter.

NAPOLEONIC HEGEMONY

Un peu de temps les temples de couleurs

De blanc & noir des deux entre meslee:

Roges & iaunes leur embleront les leurs,

Sang, terre, peste, faim, feu, d'eaue affollee.

It won't be long before differently
coloured temples

Of white and black intermingle, one with
the other

The reds and yellows will ravish all their people

Blood, land, plague, hunger, fire, rabidity.

This is a powerfully worded quatrain, which even uses the euphemism of 'maddened by water', in line four, to describe the rabid plague which overtakes the previously established order. The index date of 10 then takes us to 1810, and the seemingly inexorable rise of Napoleon Bonaparte, who has, by this time, succeeded in annexing a goodly part of Europe, and turning it into his own personal enclave, lorded over by his relatives and cronies.

SUMMARY

A Napoleonic quatrain, detailing the colours of the different countries in the tottering European order.

THE PENINSULAR WAR

Le mouvement de sens, coeur, pieds, & mains,

Seront d'accord. Naples, Leon, Secille,

Glaisves, feus, eaux: puis aux nobles Romains

Plongés, tués, mors par cerveau debile.

The movement of the senses, heart, feet, and hands

Will be in harmony. Naples, Leon, Sicily

Swords, fire, water: then are the noble Romans

Drowned, killed, dead by mental debility.

The punctuation is interesting here, as Nostradamus rarely uses either a full stop or a colon inside a sentence – he is obviously trying to get something across to us, and his use of repetition merely reinforces the admonitory aspect of the quatrain.

This is a warning, therefore, and his mention of 'harmony' in line two suggests an alchemical, as well as a purely physical, meaning. The index date of 11 would suggest the 1807-14 Peninsular War, during which the French commemorated Napoleon's 1805 victory at Austerlitz by erecting a great column on the Place Vendôme depicting Napoleon ('Naples/Leon') in the guise of Julius Caesar ('then are the noble Romans').

One year later, in 1811, the burgeoning Peninsular War saw the beginning of the end of France's European ambitions, with Napoleonic forces being defeated at Fuentes d'Onoro, in Portugal, and Albuera in Spain [see 10/11 – 1811: The Battle of Albuera], presaging further defeats by Wellington, which were to be aggravated by Napoleon's disastrous entry into Russia in 1812.

Summary

The quatrain splits into three separate parts, roughly equivalent to the yin, the yang, and the concatenation of the two – one side is harmony, the other disharmony, with the central part providing the fulcrum. According to Nostradamus there is a choice to be made – Napoleon, of whom we are clearly speaking thanks to the index date and the euphonic elision of 'Naples/Leon', makes the wrong choice.

THE BATTLE OF ALBUERA

Dessoubz lonchere du dangereux passage

Fera passer le posthume sa bande,

Les monts Pyrens passer hors son bagaige

De Parpignam courira duc à tende.

The secret amount bid on the dangerous passage

Allows the posthumous one to take his gang
through

They pass through the Pyrenees without
their baggage

From his partial engagement the duke will run
to attend them.

Both *'dessous'* and *'enchère'* in line one relate to the world of bids, auctions, and secret offers. A *dessous* is money paid underneath the table, and an *enchère* is an offer made above a previous bid – thus we have a high, but underhand, offer, which brilliantly describes the trick used by the French in their original taking of Barcelona on 29 February 1808, when Napoleon's invading force disguised itself as a convoy of wounded men.

This triggered English intervention six months later, and the index date of 11 gives us our next clue, taking us to May 1811, and the middle stages of the Peninsular War, when the Duke of Wellington won a notable series of victories over the French at Fuentes d'Onoro, in Portugal, and at Albuera, in Spain [*see* 1/11 – 1811: The Peninsular War].

SUMMARY

Despite the enormous numerical superiority of the French, the Peninsular War began to turn against them in 1811, thanks to an increase in guerrilla activity, and a scorched-earth policy on the part of the Spanish and Portuguese inhabitants and their English allies.

NAPOLEON I HOLDS VERONA

Dans peu dira faulce brute, fragile,

De bas en hault eslué promptement:

Puys en instant desloyale & labile,

Qui de Veronne aura gouvernement.

In a short time a false brute will speak, fragile

He will be raised swiftly from low to high

Then, in an instant, disloyal and imperfect

He who governs Verona.

Bearing in mind the index date of 12, this quatrain almost certainly refers to the toing and froing of Verona under Napoleon I and the Austrians between 1797 and 1814. Napoleon still controlled Verona in 1812 (after having been kicked out once already in 1798), but he was to relinquish control again following his defeat in 1814. Nostradamus, a monarchist and staunch Catholic, would have held little truck for the great man, and the term 'false brute' may well have encapsulated his opinion, as well as describing two key elements of the Antichrist.

SUMMARY

The seizing and holding of Verona by Napoleon I.

THE ABBÉ DE FOIX
& THE BONAPARTES

FEBRUARY 1812

Apparoistra aupres de Buffalorre

L'hault & procere entré dedans Milan

L'abbé de Foix avec ceux de saint Morre

Feront la forbe abillez en vilan.

He will appear near Buffalora

The high, tall one entered Milan

The abbé of Foix is with those of Saint-Maur

They will play the pirate, dressed up as peasants.

Interestingly, until the Revolution, the 'abbé de Foix' was sole master of the castle of Savignac-les-Ormeaux, which, in February 1812 (*see* index date) found itself requisitioned by the Spanish, who had occupied Ax-les-Thermes, just a few kilometres down the road. The 'high, tall one' may therefore suggest the 'jumped-up' Napoleon, who had entered Milan for his coronation on 8 May 1805, and whose fault the Spanish sequestration of Savignac undoubtedly was.

Napoleon III, however, was the only one of Napoleon Bonaparte's family to have anything directly to do with 'Buffalora' (a village situated on the main Milan road, where it crosses the Naviglio Grande), for his troops fought the Austrians over it during the 24 June 1859 Battle of Solferino. It should perhaps be mentioned here that Napoleon III was considerably taller than his uncle, Napoleon Bonaparte, but, all that notwith-standing, the quatrain seems something of a hodgepodge.

SUMMARY

It is rather hard to form a connection between the abbé de Foix and the Napoleon family, except collaterally, with the seques-tration of the abbé's old estates by the Spanish, as a direct result of the Napoleon-inspired Peninsular War of 1808–14.

THE BATTLES OF VITORIA & LEIPZIG

1813

13

4

De plus grand perte nouvelles raportées,

Le raport fait le camp s'estonnera:

Bandes unies encontre revoltées,

Double phalange grand abandonnera.

News is brought of even greater losses

The army is stunned once the report is made

Groups unite against the rebels

The great one will abandon the double phalange.

The 'great one' is Napoleon, and the year is 1813 (*see* index date) – a pivotal year in the Napoleonic era. In June, Napoleon receives news of his peninsular army's stunning defeat at the Battle of Vitoria, Spain, by British commander Arthur Wellesley (later to be made the Duke of Wellington). Later that same year, between 16 and 19 October, and thanks to a disastrous change of tactics ('the great one will abandon the double phalange'), Napoleon himself is defeated at the Battle of Leipzig (a.k.a. the Battle of the Nations).

SUMMARY

The year 1813 was a dreadful one for Napoleon, culminating in his catastrophic defeat at the Battle of Leipzig.

JEAN-BAPTISTE
BERNADOTTE

1813

13

8

Le croisé frere par amour effrenee

Fera par Praytus Bellerophon mourir,

Classe à mil ans la femme forcenee

Beu le breuvage, tous deux apres perir.

The crossed brother is unconstrained in his love

He will try to have Bellerophon killed by Proteus

The madwoman and the thousand year army

The potion drunk, both later perish.

This quatrain is imbrued with Greek myth, as we know from the mention of 'Bellerophon' and 'Proteus'. Falsely accused by Queen Eurynome of attempting to seduce her, Bellerophon is set up for death by her husband, King Proteus, and father, Iobates, King of Lycea. Sent on suicidal missions, he surmounts them all, before falling foul of Zeus's gadfly when he attempts, in his vainglory, to fly Pegasus to the top of Mount Olympus.

Could Napoleon be Proteus and Jean-Baptiste Bernadotte Bellerophon? Or vice versa? Either way, the two had a turbulent relationship, with Napoleon first creating Bernadotte a Marshal of France, and then as good as cashiering him. Bernadotte then astonished Napoleon by being elected heir to the throne of Sweden by a grateful military, and immediately switching his allegiance to his adopted country. Fearful of Napoleon's increasing vainglory, Bernadotte then allied the Swedes, in 1813, with Napoleon's enemies, preventing Marshal Ney from taking Berlin at the Battle of Dennewitz, and becoming one of Napoleon's most implacable enemies in the process.

S U M M A R Y

The fraught relationship between Jean-Baptiste Bernadotte and Napoleon Bonaparte is endlessly fascinating. Bernadotte eventually proved to be one of Napoleon's nemeses, and his descendants (despite Bernadotte's alleged sporting of a 'Death to kings!' tattoo from his Jacobin days) still hold the throne of Sweden.

THE ALLIED ADVANCE
INTO FRANCE

10 NOVEMBER 1813

Les exilez autour de la Soulongne

Conduis de nuit pour marcher à Lauxois,

Deux de Modene truculent de Bologne,

Mys descouvers par feu de Burançoys.

The exiles around Sologne

Are taken at night to walk to the Auxois

Two from Modena are truculent towards Bologna

Half uncovered by fire in Buzançais.

The 'Auxois' is a battle horse, originally from Burgundian stock, and thus it appears that we are speaking of a battle here, possibly involving mercenaries ('the exiles'). The obvious candidate is Arthur Wellesley's foray into France, where he defeated Marshal Soult at Toulouse on 10 November 1813 (*see* index date). Napoleon's collapse had actually begun a little earlier, with his defeat at the Battle of Leipzig on 16 to 19 October, and it was completed by the spring of the following year, with the allied entry into Paris.

SUMMARY

The year 1813 saw the beginning of the end for Napoleon Bonaparte, and within six months of his defeat at Leipzig the only piece of European land he was allowed to govern was Elba.

THE DUKE OF WELLINGTON

Le prince Anglois Mars à son coeur de ciel

Voudra poursuivre sa fortune prospere,

Des deux duelles l'un percera le fiel:

Hay de lui, bien aymé de sa mere.

The English prince with Mars as his celestial heart

Will wish to follow prosperous fate

Of two duels, one pierces the gall

Hated by him, much loved by his mother.

The Duke of Wellington was considered such a disaster by his mother, the Countess of Mornington, that she was heard to proclaim: 'I vow to God that I don't know what I shall do with my awkward son Arthur.' She far preferred his two older brothers.

The Iron Duke ('Mars' was the god of war) fought a famous duel in 1829, with Lord Winchilsea, in which both men fired into the air. His other duel, of course, was with Napoleon Bonaparte at the Battle of Waterloo in 1815, in which Napoleon was both 'galled' (Gauled) and defeated. Napoleon died of stomach cancer (the 'gall' again) six years later, in 1821.

SUMMARY

Set in 1816, just one year after the Duke of Wellington's victory at Waterloo, Nostradamus describes the two duels in the duke's life, and the early excoriation of the duke by his mother.

THE KINGDOM OF LOMBARDY-VENETIA

Ce qui ravy sera du ieune Milve,

Par les Normans de France & Picardie:

Les noirs du temple du lieu de Negrisilve,

Feront aulberge & feu de Lombardie.

That which is ravished by the young Hawk

By the Normans of France and Picardy

The blacks of the temple in the Black Forest

Will make an inn and a fire of Lombardy.

This is probably about the restoration of Austrian rule over Lombardy following Napoleon's defeat at Waterloo in 1815 (the 'blacks of the temple of the Black Forest' are the black-uniformed Prussians who partially engineered his defeat).

A tenuous sort of mini-state was created, called the Kingdom of 'Lombardy'-Venetia, but it was finally annexed by the Kingdom of Italy half a century later, in 1866.

SUMMARY

Napoleon was the 'young Hawk' who ravished Lombardy with his 'Normans of France and Picardy', but he was a tired old hawk by the time of the defeat at Waterloo, which returned Lombardy to the Austrian fold.

THE DEATH OF NAPOLEON BONAPARTE

5 MAY 1821

21

5

Par le trespas du monarque latin,

Ceux qu'il aura par regne secouruz:

Le feu luyra, divisé le butin,

La mort publique aux hardis incoruz.

Thanks to the death of the Latin monarch

Those he will have sheltered during his reign

The fire will shine, the booty will be divided

A public death for the bold and incorruptible.

The index date of 21 takes us directly to the death of former French emperor and King of Italy, Napoleon Bonaparte ('the Latin monarch'), on 5 May 1821, on the island of St Helena, in the South Atlantic. His followers ('those he will have sheltered during his reign') had an increasingly hard time of it after his death (interested parties might like to view Ridley Scott's film *The Duellists* for a surprisingly accurate picture of post-Napoleonic France), although Napoleon's 'fire did increasingly shine', in particular in England, where he moved from being excoriated to the attainment of quasi-heroic status as a result of the public's disenchantment with Lord Liverpool's reactionary post-war government.

SUMMARY

Both date and detail are pinpoint accurate in this quatrain, which describes the death of Napoleon Bonaparte on the British island of St Helena.

NAPOLEON BONAPARTE'S DISINTERMENT

Avant qu'advienne le changement d'empire,

Il adviendra un cas bien merveilleux,

Le champ mué, le pilier de porphyre,

Mis, translaté sus le rochier noilleux.

Before the change of empire

A marvellous circumstance will occur

The field will moult, a pillar of porphyry

Will be placed there, transforming what lies
beneath the stony rock.

The word *noyau* (whose Old French pronunciation is euphonically akin to '*noilleux*') is another word for stone, giving us stone-stone, or stone kernel. There is an astronomical link too, as *le noyau d'une comète* is the 'nucleus of a comet'. This spatial suggestion is pointed up by Nostradamus's use of the word 'marvellous' in line two, implying something out of the ordinary, or beyond the everyday.

'Porphyry' is a particularly hard form of igneous rock, which happens to be purple (the colour of royalty), and is thus also the colour of empires. An emperor born (as opposed to coming to power in a coup) was termed *porphyrogenitus*, and would be entombed in purple. This idea was continued by the Bonapartists who recovered the body of Napoleon I from St Helena in 1840, intending to immure it in a porphyry sarcophagus at Les Invalides – traditionally, however, all porphyry came from one particular quarry, the Mons Porpyritis (or Porphyry Mountain), in the Eastern Desert of Egypt, which, unfortunately, happened to be unavailable in 1840, and thus Finnish quartzite had to be used instead.

This all occurred before the 'change of empire', just as Nostradamus predicted, in the sense that the Second French Empire dates from 1852 to 1870, falling between the Second and Third Republics. The 'marvellous circumstance' thus becomes the recovery of Napoleon's remains, and his reinterment back on French soil becomes the 'transformation', of what lies beneath the stony rock into a noumenal – rather than a merely physical – monument.

SUMMARY

Napoleon holds the key to the French psyche. He may be both a winner and a loser, but when he lost, he lost with élan, and when he won, he conquered.

PART TWO

THE SECOND ANTICHRIST: ADOLF HITLER

With the arrival on the scene of Adolf Hitler, Nostradamus seems to ratchet up a notch in his depiction of pure evil. This is entirely compatible with the view that each of the three Antichrists Nostradamus offers us is due to surpass the one who came before him in horror and vile perpetrations. Hitler was born – entirely coincidentally, one assumes, although Hitler himself ascribed a certain vainglorious significance to it – on the very cusp of Easter day 1889 (Easter fell on 21 April that year, whilst Hitler's birthday fell on the 20th).

Hitler was later to take the 'cult of the infallible leader' to even further lengths than Napoleon Bonaparte ever could, hampered, as Napoleon was, by the necessity to send his signals or bruit himself abroad via only semaphore, carrier pigeon, ship, post horse, or coach. Hitler was the first Antichristian figure, therefore, to benefit from radio-based transatlantic telecommunication – a service which began in 1927, just six years before his vertiginous accession to power as German Chancellor.

Previous to that, in the run-up to the famous Beer Hall Putsch of 1923, Hitler had been significantly influenced by the Satanist, Occultist, and morphine addict, Dietrich Eckart (1868–1923), to whom he dedicated the second volume of his *Mein Kampf.* Certain commentators have attempted to play down Eckart's influence on Hitler, but there is no doubt that at his death in 1923, Eckart (a member of the ultra-secretive Thule Society) sincerely believed that he had set Hitler on a secret occult path to total power and the rule of the 'superior being', a theory which undoubtedly swayed Adolf Hitler's own views on the Aryan ascendancy (the word 'Aryan' in Sanskrit means 'noble'), and the views of his fellow occultist and propagandist henchman, Heinrich Himmler.

Eckart's last words were:

> Follow Hitler! He will dance, but it is I who have called the tune. I have initiated him into the 'Secret Doctrine', opened his centres of vision, and given him the means to communicate with the Powers. Do not mourn for me: I shall have influenced history more than any other German.

The vainglorious Eckart also schooled Hitler in the 'techniques of self-confidence, self-projection, persuasive oratory, body language and discursive sophistry' that were to stand him in such good stead in his seemingly inexorable rise to power, and which were – or would become – such powerful tools in the armoury of all three of Nostradamus's Antichrists.

These oratorical tools are best summed up by Nostradamus's own words in quatrain 3/35 – 2035, a quatrain which I have ascribed to the Birth of the Third Antichrist, but which could also apply, in roughly equal measure, to all three of the Antichrists Nostradamus pinpoints for us in his *Centuries*:

> *Du plus profond de l'Occident d'Europe,*
> *De pauvres gens un ieune enfant naistra,*
> *Qui par sa langue seduira grande troupe:*
> *Son bruit au regne d'Orient plus croistra.*

> From deep in the Western part of Europe
> A child will be born, to poor parents
> He will seduce the multitude with his tongue
> The noise of his reputation will grow in the Eastern kingdom.

ADOLF HITLER'S BIRTH CHART

Born: Saturday 20 April 1889
Time: 18.30 (LMT -1.00)
Place: Braunau am Inn, Austria
Location: 48N15 13E02

Planetary Placements

Sun in Taurus

Ascendant in Libra

Moon in Capricorn

Mercury in Aries

Venus in Taurus

Mars in Taurus

Jupiter in Capricorn

Saturn in Leo

Uranus in Libra

Neptune in Gemini

Pluto in Gemini

Midheaven in Leo

North Node in Cancer

Planetary Aspects

Sun: Trine harmonizing with Moon

Sun: Conjunct uniting with Mercury

Sun: Trine harmonizing with Jupiter

Sun: Opposition confronting Ascendant

Sun: Square challenging Midheaven

Moon: Conjunct uniting with Jupiter

Mercury: Opposition confronting Uranus

Mercury: Opposition confronting Ascendant

Venus: Conjunct uniting with Mars

Venus: Square challenging Saturn

Mars: Square challenging Saturn

Uranus: Conjunct uniting with Ascendant

Neptune: Conjunct uniting with Pluto

Neptune: Sextile cooperating with Midheaven

Pluto: Sextile cooperating with Midheaven

Astrological & Numerological Summary

According to the Chinese zodiac Adolf Hitler was born under the sign of the Ox (just as Napoleon Bonaparte was). His element was the earth (just as Napoleon Bonaparte's was). The Ox, or water buffalo, is a beast of burden, but also aggressive when roused. This year tends to produce born leaders with dogged, unbending natures, who are prepared to take extreme measures in order to retain power – such people do not tend to take prisoners, and will not tolerate criticism. The surface nature of the Ox can appear gentle and outgoing, making them attractive and influential – a virtual necessity in the run-up to power. But this calm exterior may mask an easily aroused and stubborn temper, capable of carrying all before it. Such people are often fixed in opinion, and unswerving in view – as a counter to this, they may also be highly astute in terms of meticulous planning. But they are also lazy – a trait which Hitler possessed in spades, and which made him, on occasion, a difficult man for his key advisers to gain access to.

As a Taurean (especially one with a Libra ascendant) Hitler would have been touchy and jealous of his rights – the sort of man who uses surface charm to disguise flaws in his personality. The Berghof – Hitler's mountain residence in Berchtesgaden, the traditional hunting ground of German and Bavarian monarchs – is a classic Taurean security blanket, as is the Kehlsteinhaus, or Eagle's Nest Retreat, which was designed and built for Hitler's 50th birthday by head of the Nazi Party Chancellery and Hitler's private secretary, Martin Bormann. Both are self-consciously vainglorious in intent, and greedy in inference and in their intended relation to the past. Hitler's moon in Capricorn, too, shows us a cold, self-controlled nature, aloof, and superior by default – this is the classic background of the megalomaniac (Napoleon, too, has his moon in Capricorn).

Numerologically, Adolf Hitler's name adds up to 7 under Cagliostro's kabbalistic system, which is, in turn, based on that of Cornelius Agrippa, who based his theories on the Hebrew alphabet (a rather ironical coincidence in Hitler's case): A is 1, D is 4, O is 7, L is 3, F is 8, H is 5, I is 1, T is 4, L is 3, E is 5 and R is 2, making 43, i.e. 4 + 3, which equals 7 [*see* 5/32 – 1932: The Rise of Adolf Hitler as Foretold by Kabbalism]. Seven, in this case, is a magical number, which equates very clearly with Hitler's interest in the occult (*see* my comments on Hitler's relationship with Dietrich Eckart earlier in this chapter. Sevens tend to be fascinated with all aspects of mystery and mysticism. They are also sometimes psychic, and can often be in danger of mistaking their own inner reality for its external, but significantly different, counterpart. If their worst aspects come to the fore, they can easily lose touch with reality, becoming captious, incompetent, and vague.

THE SECOND ANTICHRIST/
HITLERIAN TIMELINE

1920: Adolf Hitler states his agenda – Nostradamus claims to see the 'mark' of the beast on Hitler's 'forehead, nose, and face'.

1932: Hitler's rise is foretold by kabbalism and numerology.

1933: Adolf Hitler proclaims the beginning of the Third Reich. Nostradamus correlates Hitler's own chosen title of *der Führer* with the Old French term, *Guyon*, also meaning a guide or a leader.

Hitler threatens Austria. It is clear that storm clouds are looming.

1934: The Stavisky affair arguably weakened France, leaving her more vulnerable than previously, and alerting Hitler to what he thought of as her 'decadence' and 'corruption'.

Hitler eradicates his competitors and consolidates his power in the infamous Night of the Long Knives.

1935: Benito Mussolini achieves governmental control of Italy, giving Adolf Hitler an early and crucial ally in the heartland of southern Europe.

1936: Generalissimo Franco becomes a second, equally
       crucial ally of Adolf Hitler's.

       Franco's Nationalist forces (including the Carlists,
       the Legitimist monarchists, and the Fascist Falange)
       relieve the Alcazar, further reinforcing Fascist
       domination of southern Europe.

       Adolf Hitler 'reoccupies' the Rhineland, using, as his
       excuse, that he is saving German speakers and
       German-speaking communities from foreign
       domination.

       King Edward VIII abdicates his throne, reinforcing
       Hitler's view that his major potential enemies in
       Europe are busy weakening themselves, whilst he is
       secretly rearming and re-strengthening Germany.

       Hitler intends the 1936 Berlin Summer Olympics as a
       'switch' to beat the decadent Western Powers with.
       Via propaganda, he seeks to turn the Olympic Games
       into an advertisement for Aryan supremacy.

1938: Adolf Hitler annexes Austria, instantly enlarging the
       German bailiwick, and providing himself with an
       ample new source of potential Nazi recruits.

       The Anglo/Italian Pact further reinforces Hitler's
       views about the weakness and capacity for havering
       of the Western Powers and the League of Nations.

1939:   Much to Hitler's joy, Spain's General Franco joins
        the Anti-Comintern Pact, uniting Spain, Japan,
        Germany, and Italy against the Communist
        International. This can now, in retrospect, be seen as
        a prefatory move towards the Second World War, in
        which only Spain was to hold back on active partici-
        pation in the conflict, despite Hitler's entreaties.

        Germany and Italy cement the infamous Pact
        of Steel, in which Mussolini acknowledges that
        henceforward Germany's enemies will be Italy's
        enemies too.

        General Gustave Gamelin makes a fatal tactical error
        in his over-reliance on the capacity of the flawed (and
        bypassable) Maginot Line to stop any German
        advance into France.

1939–45: Hitler finds himself facing a somewhat larger
        Northern Wartime Alliance than he had initially
        counted on.

1940:   Hitler wins the Battle of France. He seems unstop-
        pable. In many ways he has reached the height of his
        power.

        Hitler unleashes the London Blitz in a bid to force
        the United Kingdom out of the war. Nostradamus
        describes the destruction caused by Hermann
        Goering's Luftwaffe.

1941: King Christian X of Denmark defies Adolf Hitler, and comes to represent the spirit of Danish resistance to Nazi occupation.

Erwin Rommel's rise and fall is encapsulated in a single, brilliant, quatrain, representing also the first signs of a moral backlash against Hitlerian rule.

Adolf Hitler's actions threaten the fabric of medieval Europe. Nostradamus compares the 'pagan' Adolf Hitler unfavourably to Charlemagne, whose legacy he has put at risk. The British, aware of Aachen's Carolingian importance as a symbol of a unified Europe, endeavour to spare its cathedral.

1943: Even tiny Monaco is occupied, first by the Italians, and then by the Germans.

Adolf Hitler's actions lead directly to the carpet-bombing of Germany and Occupied France, resulting in the virtual destruction of Old Europe.

By the end of 1943, the tide of war is beginning to turn in the Allies' favour.

1944: American parachutists land near the town of Fréjus, on what was later to be called the Riviera D-Day.

Nostradamus highlights Pope Pius XII, and his problematic position vis-à-vis the Allies.

The key port of Calais is besieged, and then liberated, by a combined Czech/Canadian force.

1945: The classic Adolf Hitler quatrain, encompassing the final catastrophic year of the Second World War.

The year 1945 sees the downfall of Adolf Hitler's Third Reich, and, with it, the demise of the second of Nostradamus's three Antichrists.

THE HITLERIAN
QUATRAINS

ADOLF HITLER PROCLAIMS HIS AGENDA

Freres et soeurs en divers lieux captifs

Se trouveront passer pres du monarque:

Les contempler ses rameaux ententifs,

Desplaisant voir menton, front, nez, les marques.

Brothers and sisters held captive in various places

They pass near the monarch

He looks at them with alert attention

It is disagreeable to see the marks on forehead, nose, and face.

When Nostradamus speaks of 'marks', in line four, it is more than likely that he is referring to the 'mark of the beast' (ergo the mark of the devil), i.e. 666 – or 616 or 665, depending on which source you use – as defined in Revelations xiii: 18:

> Here is wisdom. Let him that hath understanding count the number of the beast: for it is the number of a man; and his number *is* Six hundred threescore *and* six.

Many consider the number to be an example of Hebrew *gematria* (numerology), which was often used to disguise the 'revealed' rather than the 'mystical' (i.e. the kabbalistic) form of a name (be it that of the Antichrist, or that of a Roman emperor, like Nero, who was considered a roughly similar order of threat by the Jews).

As it is likely that Nostradamus considered Adolf Hitler to be the second Antichrist, we must look to 1920 (given the index date of 20, which does not correspond so easily to Napoleon) for an explanation of this quatrain. And in February 1920 we find that Hitler presented his National Socialist agenda for the first time in Munich. This agenda was heavily based on the writings of Martin Luther (particularly on his treatise entitled *On The Jews And Their Lies* 1543), in which Luther proclaimed the following:

> The reason why I did not then perceive the absurdity of such an illusion [i.e. of considering Jews as ordinary human beings] was that the only

external mark which I recognized as distinguishing them from us was the practice of their strange religion.

S U M M A R Y

Adolf Hitler based much of his excoriation of the Jews on the writings of Martin Luther (who was anathema to Nostradamus). In 1920 the first detailed postulation of a National Socialist political philosophy was put forward, which was later to lead to the Holocaust.

THE RISE OF ADOLF HITLER AS FORETOLD BY KABBALISM

DATE

1932

NOSTRADAMUS'S INDEX DATE

32

CENTURY NUMBER

5

Ou tout bon est, tout bien Soleil & Lune,

Est abondant sa ruyne s'approche:

Du ciel s'advance varier ta fortune,

En mesme estat que la septiesme roche.

Where all is good, all is well with the
sun and moon

The abundant east, its ruin approaches

Advancing from the sky to alter your fortune

In the same state as the seventh rock.

'Seven' is the holy number – the 'moon', too, has seven phases, just as there are seven bodies in alchemy, with the 'Sun' representing gold, the 'Moon' – silver, Mars – iron, Mercury – quicksilver, Jupiter – tin, Venus – copper, and Saturn – lead. There are seven senses, seven deadly sins, seven virtues, and seven spirits of God. There were seven days in creation, seven graces, seven days needed for Levitical purification, seven wise masters, and seven great champions of Christendom. The upsetting, disharmonization, or transmutation of the number seven is contraindicative to world peace. In the seventh month of 1932 (*see* index date), Adolf Hitler's National Socialist Party became, for the first time ever, the largest single party in the Reichstag. Hitler had seven doctors, seven key disciples, seven major death camps – in 1932, Hindenburg's seven-year term as President of Germany came to a close. These sorts of things are bread and meat to numerologists (*see* Astrological & Numerological Summary for Adolf Hitler).

SUMMARY

A wondrously convoluted quatrain in which Nostradamus uses kabbalism to warn the world of the coming of Adolf Hitler.

ADOLF HITLER'S DECLARATION OF THE THIRD REICH

15 MARCH 1933

33

9

Hercules Roy de Rome & d'Annemarc,

De Gaule trois Guion surnommé,

Trembler l'Italie & l'unde de sainct Marc,

Premier sur tous monarque renommé.

King Hercules of Rome and Mark Anthony

Three leaders of France are surnamed Guyon

Italy and the location of Saint Marc will tremble

First amongst all is the monarch's renown.

Let's dissect this quatrain a little: there never was a 'Hercules' who was king of 'Rome' and of Denmark, so we are talking of a 'Herculean' figure here, and not an eponymous king – in addition the 'Denmark/d'Annemarc' clue seems a false one, as we know that Mark Antony ('annemarc' reversed) became obsessed by Hercules, and even gave Hercules a fictional son, Anton, from whom he claimed ancestry. 'Guyon' is a well-known and prestigious name in France (as well as meaning a guide, a leader, or a chief in Old French). It has belonged to soldiers (General Claude Guyon), scientists (Félix Guyon, the father of urology in France), actors (Alexandre Guyon), and politicians (Jean Guyon). It has even belonged to Quietist mystics (Jeanne de la Motte-Guyon). In line three *'unde'* comes from the Latin, and means 'from whence', which, in the context of 'St Mark's', usually means Venice.

So we are speaking of strong, nay even Herculean leaders, sharing an index date of 33. Albrecht von Wallenstein in 1633? Augustus the Strong of Poland, who died in 1733, triggering the War of the Polish Succession? Or is this more sinister, relating to the declaration, by Adolf Hitler, of the Third Reich, on 15 March 1933 (remember that Hitler was known as *der Führer*, meaning a guide or leader – the same as Guyon). Hitler/der Führer/Guyon became the leader of France, and he also made Italy, Rome, and Venice (St Mark's) tremble.

SUMMARY

The Sherlock Holmes touch was needed for this quatrain, but we got there in the end, with the Guyon/Führer connection leading us straight to Adolf Hitler's declaration of the Third

Reich on 15 March 1933 – and just like Hercules and Mark Antony, Hitler finally succumbed to vainglory and monomania. Unlike Hercules, however, he was not summoned up to heaven on a cloud.

STORM CLOUDS LOOM OVER AUSTRIA

En la cité où le loup entrera,

Bien pres de là les ennemis seront:

Copie estrange grand païs gastera.

Aux murs & Alpes les amis passeront.

In the city which the wolf enters

There, nearby, will the enemy be

A foreign army will swallow the great country

Friends will cross both walls and Alps.

Given the index date of 33, this is clearly about Adolf Hitler's long-term plans for Austria, which were facilitated by the German Federal elections of 5 March 1933, in which Hitler's National Socialists won 44 per cent of the vote. Following Austrian Chancellor Engelbert Dolfuss's panic-stricken decision to suspend parliament and give himself dictatorial powers, the inevitable pro-Nazi riots broke out in Vienna, predating a virtual civil war. Dolfuss was assassinated on 25 July 1934 by eight home-grown Nazis intent on a coup, and, after numerous other outrages, Austria was duly annexed by – or merged with – Germany's Third Reich (depending, of course, on your point of view) less than four years later, on 12 March 1938 [*see* 1/38 – 1938: Adolf Hitler's Annexation of Austria]. The Anschluss followed an extensive '*Heim in Reich*' campaign, in which Hitler attempted to persuade any person of German extraction still living outside Germany that their country should, by rights, be part of a Greater Germany.

Summary

A clear, concise, and index-date-perfect quatrain highlighting the seemingly inevitable merger between Austria and Germany in the already inflammatory environment of the 1930s.

THE STAVISKY AFFAIR

8 JANUARY 1934

L'oyseau de proye volant a la fenestre

Avant conflict faict aux Francoys pareure

L'un bon prendra, l'un ambigue sinistre,

La partie foyble tiendra par bon augure.

The bird of prey flying at the window

Appears to the French before the conflict commences

Some will take it favourably, others as a sinister cold collation

The weaker side will hold fast and gain the ascendancy.

'*Ambigue*' can have two possible definitions here (surprise, surprise) – one is 'ambiguous', and the other is a 'cold supper' or 'cold collation'. The second appears to be Nostradamus's meaning, bearing in mind his use of the word 'take' (as in the taking of food) in the first part of the line. Given this fact, and the categorical mention of 'the French' in line two, together with the multitude of other clues and an index date of 34, we are inexorably led towards the Stavisky Affair, which reached its climax on 8 January 1934.

Handsome Serge Alexandre Stavisky (*le beau Sasha*), an embezzler and dealer in fraudulent bonds, apparently committed suicide in an upper room of a Chamonix chalet following 7 years of claim, counterclaim, and cover-up (he was granted bail on 19 separate occasions) by the governing French Radical-Socialist government. The alleged suicide by gunshot was widely viewed as an assassination plot by the police designed to protect high-up officials implicated in the ongoing scandal, however, and both the royalist right and the communist left took to the streets in protest during the Paris riots of 6 and 7 February, which culminated in a crippling general strike.

Stavisky's crime was to have released hundreds of millions of francs' worth of false bonds to the City of Bayonne's municipal pawnshop – bonds that were subsequently repurchased by a series of life insurance companies which, according to Janet Flanner, the *New Yorker*'s Paris correspondent, 'were counselled by the Minister of Colonies, who was counselled by the Minister of Commerce, who was counselled by the Mayor of Bayonne, who was counselled by the little manager of the hockshop, who was counselled by Stavisky'.

One would like to think that the 'bird of prey flying at the window' in line one represents the *flics* (cops), who constituted what certain newspapers of the period chose to call Stavisky's 'long arm' – a jocular reference to the distance the bullet had allegedly travelled before finishing off the no doubt somewhat reluctant suicidee.

Summary

Nostradamus's take on the famous Stavisky Affair, which engendered a series of riots, a putsch, and a general strike, whose ultimate result was the downfall of an unpopular and corrupt French government.

THE NIGHT OF THE LONG KNIVES

DATE

30 JUNE 1934

NOSTRADAMUS'S INDEX DATE
34
CENTURY NUMBER
8

Apres victoire du Lyon au Lyon

Sur la montaigne de IURA Secatombe

Delues & brodes septieme million

Lyon, Ulme à Mausol mort & tombe.

After the victory of the lion over the lion

There will be oath-taking in the mountain
hecatomb

The deluge and embroidery of the seventh million

Lion, Ulm to the Mausoleum, death and tomb.

The two 'lions' are Adolf Hitler and Ernst Röhm, and Hitler chose the night of 30 June 1934 as the occasion on which to bring Röhm, and his out-of-control SA (SA-hecatomb, ergo 'Secatombe') to heel, via Operation Hummingbird. Eighty-five died in the purge, with thousands more arrested. Röhm, after refusing to take his own life, was executed at Stadelheim prison two days later. The 'oath-taking on the mountain' is that of the now resurgent SS at Schloss Wewelsburg, their spiritual home, and the mention of the 'seventh million' in line three, alongside the 'deluge', and the 'embroidery' (Jewish bodies are covered with a hand-sewn cloth similar to that worn by the high priest in the temple at Yom Kippur), represents the approximate number of Jews killed during the whole of World War Two as part of Hitler's so-called Final Solution.

SUMMARY

An extraordinary quatrain, clearly anticipating the future horrors of World War Two – horrors which became inevitable following Hitler's consolidation of power during the Night of the Long Knives.

BENITO MUSSOLINI CONTROLS ITALY

1935

35

4

Le feu estaint, les vierges trahiront

La plus grand part de la bande nouvelle:

Fouldre à fer, lance les seulz roy garderont:

Etrusque & Corse, de nuict gorge allumelle.

The fire is extinguished, the virgins have betrayed it

The greater part of the new group

Iron casks, priests will watch over the king
with lances

Etruria and Corsica, throats cut by night.

Line one is pretty clearly about the vestal 'virgins', whose job it was to guard the 'undying fire' of the sacred vestal flame – for if it went out, Rome would be in danger. Given the index date of 35, the 'new group' is certainly the National Fascist Party of Benito Mussolini, which, by 1935, had cemented governmental control of Italy. Mussolini also sidelined both King Victor Emmanuel III (who mistrusted the Axis, preferring traditional ties with England and France) and Pope Pius XI (who attacked the Fascist regime in his *Non Abbiamo Bisogno* encyclical). Nostradamus's predictions for Italy, and the consequences inherent in the extinguishing of the vestal flame, would later be proved true, with Rome falling, first to the Axis, and then to the Allies.

SUMMARY

This quatrain is about Benito Mussolini's domination of Italy – by 1935, for instance, 75 per cent of Italian businesses were under state control, and it had become increasingly obvious that Mussolini intended to align himself, not with Italy's traditional allies, France and England, but with Adolf Hitler's Germany.

GENERALISSIMO FRANCO

De castel Franco sortira l'assemblee

L'ambassadeur non plaisant fera scisme

Ceux de Ribiere seront en la meslee

Et au grand goulphre desnier ont l'entrée.

Franco will force the assembly out of Castile

The outraged ambassador will create a schism

Rivera's men will form part of the free-for-all

The leader will be refused entry to the gulf.

This is one of the most famous of all Nostradamus's quatrains, for it mentions the names of both Francisco 'Franco' (1892–1975), self-proclaimed Caudillo de España, *por la gracia de Dios*, and Primo de 'Rivera' (1870–1930), Franco's marginally less dictatorial predecessor. When Rivera died, his son, José Antonio, recreated the Falange movement in his father's honour, fighting alongside Franco during the Spanish Civil War of 1936–39. Franco became dictator of Spain in 1936 following the cessation of hostilities, and remained in control for a further 36 years. The mention of the 'outraged ambassador' in line two undoubtedly refers to the sequence of foreign interventions that were to mark the period of the Spanish Civil War, and that included the German carpet-bombing of Guernica, and the last line refers to the 1936 Spanish Republican Government's exile of Franco to the Canary Islands, thus effectively denying him entry to the Mediterranean 'gulf'. The Spanish would later have reason to look on Rivera's benevolent autocracy with nostalgic fondness, given the unremittingly severe dictatorship that ensued.

Summary

A brilliantly successful quatrain mentioning both Francisco Franco and his predecessor, Primo de Rivera.

THE RELIEF OF THE ALCAZAR

DATE
1936

NOSTRADAMUS'S INDEX DATE
15
CENTURY NUMBER
9

Pres de Parpan les rouges detenus,
Ceux du milieu parfondrez menez loing:
Trois mis en pieces, & cinq mal soustenus,
Pour le Seigneur & Prelat de Bourgoing.

The reds are held prisoner near Perpignan

The middle classes are fused and taken far

Three are torn to pieces, and five are starved

For the lord and prelate of Burgos.

All the respective index dates of 15 have been tried here (1615, 1715, 1815, etc.), and still the quatrain looks as though it refers to the Spanish Civil War of 1936–39. The 'lord and prelate of Burgos' would therefore be General Franco (pro-clerical), as Burgos was one of the original cities to fall to the army uprising in 1936, under General Emilio Mola – Franco later made it his headquarters. 'Perpignan', too, conforms to Nostradamus's 'red' (communist) stereotype, as it represented the border between France and Republican Spain, and was (and still is) the home of many Republican (i.e. anti-clerical) refugees – the town itself is in large part of Spanish origin, and only became French in 1659. The reference to 'starvation' in the text may refer to Franco's famous relief of the Alcazar Citadel in Toledo, which delayed the Nationalist attack on Madrid.

SUMMARY

This quatrain would appear to refer to the Spanish Civil War, with particular reference to the Nationalists at Burgos, and the Republican diaspora at Perpignan.

ADOLF HITLER'S REOCCUPATION OF THE RHINELAND

DATE
1936

NOSTRADAMUS'S INDEX DATE
36

CENTURY NUMBER
10

Apres le Roi du soucq guerres parlant,

L'isle Harmotique le tiendra à mespris,

Quelque ans bons rongeant un & pillant

Par tyrranie à l'isle changeant pris.

After the King of the markets speaks of war

The United Island holds him in contempt

For a few good years one man gnaws and pillages

The island changes its mind because of his tyranny.

The year 1936 saw Adolf Hitler defying the terms of the Treaty of Versailles and reoccupying the Rhineland. Since his rise to the chancellorship of Germany in 1933, the United Kingdom (the 'United Islands') had paid scant attention to Hitler, viewing him as little more than a tin-pot tyrant. This allowed Hitler to continue with his secret plans for rearmament, only really coming into the open with the Anschluss of Austria [see 1/38 – 1938: Adolf Hitler's Annexation of Austria]. The expression *Markt König* in German ('king of the markets') implies a jumped-up or socially ambitious man from a humble background – a description which fitted Adolf Hitler to a tee.

SUMMARY

The secret rise of Adolf Hitler, encouraged by the tendency towards appeasement shown by a succession of United Kingdom governments.

KING EDWARD VIII ABDICATES HIS THRONE

11 DECEMBER 1936

36

2

Du grand Prophete les letres seront prinses
Entre les mains du tyran deviendront:
Frauder son roy seront ses entreprinses,
Mais ses rapines bien tost le troubleront.

The letters are taken by the great Prophet

They will come into the hands of the tyrant

He will endeavour to defraud his king

But his robberies will soon cause him trouble.

The index date of 36 inevitably takes us to 3 December 1936, and to the breaking of silence by the British press ('the great Prophet') on the subject of King Edward VIII's infatuation with Mrs Wallis Simpson. The 'tyrant' is Stanley Baldwin, who made it clear to the king that he could not marry a twice-divorced woman and hope to continue on as King of England. The king broadcast his decision to abdicate on 11 December, and Baldwin retired from his Prime Ministership less than five months later.

SUMMARY

A categorical, index-date-perfect quatrain, detailing the run-up to the United Kingdom's 1936 abdication crisis.

THE 1936 BERLIN SUMMER OLYMPICS

Les ieux nouveau en Gaule redresses,

Après victoire de l'Insubre champaigne:

Monts d'Esperie, les grands liés, troussés:

De peur trembler la Romaigne & l'Espaigne.

The new games are as a straightened switch

After the victory of the Insubrian campaign

The Western Mountains, the great tied and bound

Both Spain and Romania tremble in fear.

Line one sees Nostradamus having great fun punning on the word '*Gaule*', which can mean either 'France', or a 'pole' or 'switch' – the word '*redresses*' provides us with our clue to the pun, however, for to *redresser un baton* is common French usage for 'to straighten a stick', and leads us to the notion of the bundled sticks, known as fasces, with which the Romans preceded any triumph or communal games, and which were symbolically used throughout 20th-century fascism (particularly in the case of the Italo/'Insubrians', where Mussolini's Fascist Party used the fasces as its main symbol).

The notion of 'new games', too, is a powerful one, as Paris hosted the Olympic Games of 1900 and 1924, and in 1936 (*see* index date), those games were handed over to Berlin, which, subsequent to the initial allocation of the games (which occurred, pre-Hitler, in 1931), now housed the German Fascist Party. The year 1936 saw fascism on the rise in both Romania and in Spain, where the Civil War was to break out on 17 July, just two weeks before the 1 August formal opening ceremony for the summer Olympics.

SUMMARY

A remarkable quatrain depicting the 1936 Berlin summer Olympics as linked to the rise of fascism and to the temporary stultification of the Western Powers – Nostradamus's image of those same powers 'tied and bound', with the Olympics functioning as a 'switch' to beat them with, is a memorable one.

ADOLF HITLER'S ANNEXATION OF AUSTRIA

12/13 MARCH 1938

Le sol et l'aigle au victeur paroistront:

Response vaine au vaincu l'on asseure,

Par cor ne crys harnois n'arresteront,

Vindicte, paix par mors si acheve à l'heure.

The sun and the eagle will appear to the victor

Empty replies reassure the loser

Neither horn nor wailing will stop them

Prosecution, and peace achieved through death.

This verse begins rather badly, but then ends on a definite upbeat, and one gets the impression that Nostradamus is looking a long way ahead for a solution to the problems triggered by 'the victor', Adolf Hitler. For given the index date of 38, and the content of the quatrain, it would seem next to certain that he is pointing to the 1938 Anschluss of Austria, during which the spiritual home of the old Hapsburg empire became, whether she liked it or not, a part of Greater Germany.

A plebiscite held the following month appeared to give the Austrian version of Hitler's National Socialist Party 99.73 per cent of the popular vote, but then the Anschluss was by that time a foregone conclusion, and few people would have been brave enough or foolhardy enough, at that particular point in history, to risk poking their heads even a fraction above the parapet.

The 'eagle' in line one is, of course, the two-headed eagle, traditional emblem of both Prussia (representing Germany) and Imperial Austria, and stems from the Emperor Charlemagne, who was, like Hitler, renowned for his ambitions vis à vis a centralized European state (the first head of the eagle stands for judicial power, whilst the second head stands for global status and imperial ambitions). The 'sun' is most likely to be a reference to the famous saying of Alexander the Great – a man to whom Hitler frequently compared himself – uttered when he was offered peace terms by Darius before the Battle of Arbela (331 BC): 'Heaven cannot support two suns, nor earth two masters.'

The single word 'prosecution' in line four is also tantalizing, and tempts one to suggest the 1945–9 Nuremberg trials, in which what remained of the Nazi hierarchy were publicly prosecuted for crimes against humanity, whilst the 'peace achieved through death' would appear to be a reference to the unconditional surrender of Germany which followed hard upon the heels of Hitler's 1945 suicide in the command bunker that underlay the Reichskanzlei gardens.

Summary

This is a somewhat long-tailed quatrain, suggesting solutions as well as problems to Hitler's insane megalomania. Always a realist, Nostradamus proves himself something of an optimist, too, in the quasi-holistic view he takes of Hitler's 1938 annexation of Austria.

THE ANGLO/ITALIAN PACT

Au profligés de paix les ennemis,

Apres avoir l'Italie superee:

Noir sanguinaire, rouge sera commis,

Feu, sang verser, eaue de sang couloree.

The enemies of the discomfiters of peace

After having Italy supreme

The black one bloody, the red will be committed

Fire, spilled blood, water coloured by blood.

'*Profligés*' is not an Old French word but a Latin one, *profligo*, meaning to 'dash down', to 'rout' or to 'discomfit', which gives the line the exact opposite meaning to the one an English speaker might instinctively ascribe to it. That said, the quatrain would seem to be about the Anglo/Italian pact of 16 April 1938 (*see* index date) in which British Prime Minister Neville Chamberlain continued on his route of appeasement, this time with Abyssinia as the postpartum victim ('the black one bloody'). For in exchange for a nominal troop withdrawal from Spain, Chamberlain accepted Italy's annexation of Abyssinia (modern-day Ethiopia) and withdrew sanctions, tacitly condoning an invasion (1935–6) that had been so unequal in its balance, and so dastardly in its use of superior weapons and mustard gas to overcome a medievally armed enemy, that it had engendered almost universal condemnation by right-thinking individuals.

SUMMARY

The Second Italo-Abyssinian War had exposed the weaknesses inherent in the League of Nations, and the Anglo/Italian pact of 1938 did nothing to either rectify matters, or to entice Mussolini away from his dangerous flirtation with Nazi Germany.

THE RUN-UP TO THE SECOND WORLD WAR

DATE

1939

NOSTRADAMUS'S INDEX DATE

39

CENTURY NUMBER

2

Un an devant le conflict Italique,

Germain, Gaulois, Hespaignols pour le fort:

Cherra l'escolle maison de republique,

Ou, hors mis peu, seront suffoqués morrs.

One year before the Italian conflict

German, French, Spanish for the fort

The Republican schoolhouse will be abused

Where, save for a few, they will be smothered to death.

This is a case of '*cherchez la guerre*' (as opposed to *la femme*). The 'Italian conflict' which Nostradamus describes as occurring a year after the index date of 39 (*see* line one), has to be the 10 June 1940's declaration of war by the Italians against France and Britain. This then carries us back to 1939, and the Nationalist takeover of Barcelona ('the Republican schoolhouse will be abused'), followed, two months later, by General Franco's seizure of Madrid, which marked the end of the Spanish Civil War and the joining, by Franco, of the Anti-Comintern Pact, uniting Spain, Japan, Germany, and Italy, against the Communist International. By 30 August 1939, the French were already evacuating their women and children from Paris. War was declared on 3 September.

SUMMARY

A splendid quatrain, index-date-accurate, and correctly describing the run-up to the declaration of the Second World War.

THE PACT OF STEEL

1939

39

3

Les sept en trois mis en concorde

Pour subiuguer des alpes Appenines:

Mais la tempeste et Ligure couarde

Les profligent en subites ruines.

The seven in three are in agreement

To subjugate the Apennines

But the weather, and cowardly Liguria

Force them into sudden ruin.

In the year 1939, Italy made many decisions which were to come home to roost during the succeeding 'seven' years. One such decision was made by Mussolini on 22 May, when the Pact of Steel was signed, cementing a ten-year friendship alliance with Adolf Hitler's Germany. This indirectly allowed Nizzardo Italians (themselves descendants of an ancient Ligurian tribe), to retake control of Nice from the French (modern-day Liguria forms part of the northern Italian Apennine Alps, roughly following the curve of the Gulf of Genoa as far as Spezia). In 1947, as a result of the wartime Italian capitulation, Nice, Briga and Tenda were returned to France, causing a quarter of the Nizzardo Italians to return to Liguria from the area around Val di Roia.

SUMMARY

The infamous Pact of Steel, in which Mussolini agreed that Germany's enemies would henceforth be Italy's enemies too.

GENERAL GUSTAVE GAMELIN

1939

39

7

Le conducteur de l'armée Francoise,

Cuidant perdre le principal phalange:

Par sus pavé de livaigne & d'ardoise,

Soy parfondra par Gennes gent estrange.

The leader of the French army

Thinking he would lose his principal phalanx

Upon a paving of grain and slate

Will fuse Genoa with an alien people.

France, alongside England, declared war on Germany on 3 September 1939, following Germany's unprovoked invasion of Poland two days before. The French army consisted of 900,000 enlisted men at the time, with a further 5,000,000 reservists, and its leader, General Gustave Gamelin, staked all on the defensive capacities of the fortified Maginot Line, twinned with an intended offensive through Belgium and the Netherlands (the Dyle Plan). In the event, the Germans attacked further south than Gamelin had anticipated, neutralizing the Maginot Line. Following the catastrophic defeat of 1940 (which did, indeed, 'fuse Genoa', ergo Italy, 'with an alien people', ergo Germany), Gamelin was removed from office in favour of General Maxime Weygand.

SUMMARY

A categorical and index-date-perfect rendition of the run-up to the Franco-German armistice of 25 June 1940 [see 9/40 – 1940: The Battle of France].

THE NORTHERN WARTIME ALLIANCE

La gent de Dace, d'Angleterre & Palonne

Et de Bohesme feront nouvelle ligue:

Pour passer outre d'Hercules la colonne,

Barcins, Tyrrens dresser cruelle brigue.

The people of Dacia, England and Poland

And of Bohemia will make a new league

In order to pass beyond Hercules's column

The Barcelonans and Tyrrhenians mount a cruel plot.

Ancient 'Dacia' covered an enormous area, encompassing all or part of Romania, Moldova, Bulgaria, Hungary and the Ukraine – 'Bohemia' takes in most of the Czech Republic, Moravia and Silesia. These countries, according to Nostradamus, together with 'England' and 'Poland' (part of which was incorporated into Bohemia anyway), join up to pass beyond the Straits of Gibraltar ('Hercules's Column').

Well it's obviously not the Crimean War (1853–56) that we're talking about, and neither does the index date fit the Second World War, which did indeed pit the 'Tyrrhenian' Italians (literally) and the 'Barcelonan' Spanish (nominally) against an alliance of most, if not all, of the other states mentioned. And yet nothing else remotely fits. So we shall have to assume that Nostradamus got his index date six years out, and that he was describing the northern allies versus Fascist Spain and Italy.

SUMMARY

A mildly unsatisfactory quatrain, although Nostradamus has his geographical parameters down to a tee in his description of the Northern Alliance. Franco's Spain remained technically neutral, of course, during the Second World War, while covertly sympathizing with the German cause.

THE BATTLE OF FRANCE

10 MAY 1940

40

9

Pres de Quintin dans la forest bourlis,

Dans l'abbaye seront Flamens ranches,

Les deux puisnais de coups my estourdis

Suitte oppressee & garde tous aches.

Near Quintin in the confused forest

Flemish will be butchered in the abbey

The youngest two are stunned by blows

The rest are overwhelmed and the guard all axed.

'*Bourlis*' is an interesting word, and has caused much head-scratching to Nostradamus commentators over the centuries. French lexicographer Pierre Augustin Boissier de Sauvages (1710–95) suggests, in his *Dictionaire Languedocien-Français*, that the word implies trouble or confusion, and stems from the Old French *bourlos*, meaning mockery – and it is true that Nostradamus was never above sacrificing lexicographical accuracy to a good rhyme. This would afford the quatrain a Dante-esque link, for Canto 1 of the *Inferno* begins: 'In the middle of life's journey I found myself in a dark forest wherein the straight way was lost.' Ergo a 'confused forest'?

The index date of 40 gives us our clue here, for it refers to 10 May 1940, when German forces invaded the Low Countries, and the Battle of France effectively began. By 28 May, Belgium was forced to capitulate, with the end of the Dunkirk evacuation taking place on 4 June. By 15 June Verdun (site of the famous 'abbey') had fallen to German forces, and by 22 June the whole of Flemish France was overwhelmed.

SUMMARY

The Battle of France, with particular emphasis on the German invasion of the Low Countries, culminating in the loss of Verdun.

THE LONDON BLITZ

1940

Le grand theatre se viendra redresser:
Le dez géte, & les retz ia tendus.
Trop le premier en glaz viendra lasser,
Par arcs prostraits de long temps ia fendus.

The great theatre will be rebuilt

The dice are thrown and the nets tightened

The first one tires too much on hearing the
death knell

Exhausted by arches that are already split.

Given the first two lines, this 'great theatre' sounds a little like a casino, a gaming room, or an opera house. If it wasn't for the index date of 40, this would seem to relate to the 1996 destruction, and 2004 reincarnation, of the Teatro la Fenice in Venice. Instead, it may be seen to refer to the London Blitz, which began on 7 September 1940, and which saw the destruction of numerous theatres (the Little, the Queens, the Shaftesbury, and the New Royalty theatres spring to mind). The 'dice are thrown' might then relate to the Battle of Britain, during which the future of the war, and of Britain's successful part in it, hung in the balance.

SUMMARY

An odd little quatrain, which seems to be portraying the 1940 London Blitz, and the destruction of some of her great theatres.

KING CHRISTIAN X
OF DENMARK
& ADOLF HITLER

1941

41

6

Le second chef du regne Dannemarc.

Par ceulx de Frise & l'isle Britannique,

Fera despendre plus de cent mille marc,

Vain exploicter voyage en Italique.

The second leader of the kingdom of Denmark

Thanks to those of Friesland and the British Isles

Will spend more than a hundred thousand marks

Vainly exploiting the journey to Italy.

Given the index date of 41, it is reasonable to assume that this quatrain refers to the Second World War, and to 'Denmark's' long-term occupation by the Axis forces (Germany and 'Italy'), dating from the Weserübung invasion of 9 April 1940. 'Friesland' (part of Holland) was also occupied, as both countries (Denmark and the Netherlands) had borders with Germany.

The invasion of Denmark was carried out with remarkably little loss of life, for King Christian X and his ministers decided that it would be inconceivable to allow the Luftwaffe to bomb Copenhagen unnecessarily. King Christian X made his disdain for the Nazi authorities clear from the start, and the 'second leader of the kingdom of Denmark' would then be Adolf Hitler, with whom the resolutely old-school king soon fell out.

Both Denmark and Friesland were instinctively pro-British, and the final two lines are probably purely symbolic of Hitler's inability to capture the hearts and minds of his unwilling subjects – a resistance that led to sabotage and to industrial action, at immense cost to the German wartime exchequer.

SUMMARY

The distinctly arms-length relationship between King Christian X of Denmark and Adolf Hitler led to King Christian's personification as the symbol of Danish resistance to Nazi occupation.

ERWIN ROMMEL

1941

Esleu sera Renad, ne sonnant mot,

Faisant le saint public vivant pain d'orge,

Tyrannizer apres tant à un cop,

Mettant à pied des plus grans sus la gorge.

The fox will be elected, without saying a word

Made into a saint by the public, he lives on
barley bread

He will be tyrannized some time later after a coup

The great ones trampling on his throat.

A splendid quatrain, in which the index date of 41 and the codeword 'fox' in line one take us directly to the year 1941, and to the victories of Erwin Rommel, nicknamed the Desert 'Fox'.

By 15 April that year Rommel had secured the whole of Libya, a success that resulted in his 'election', in August, to the role of Commander Panzer Group Afrika. Curiously enough the word 'fox' was to reappear again in Rommel's life when his car was strafed, and Rommel seriously injured, by an RCAF Spitfire piloted by Charley Fox (Charley is the rural nickname for a fox in England, so the pilot was in fact 'Foxy Fox'!).

Nostradamus then describes the upshot of the 'coup' against Adolf Hitler which was to cost Rommel his life ('some time later'), when his superiors forced him to commit suicide ('the great ones trampling on his throat').

SUMMARY

A choice quatrain focusing on 'Desert Fox' Erwin Rommel in the year of his greatest successes. Three years later his superiors forced him to commit suicide after he may – or may not – have been involved in the 20 July assassination plot against the Führer. He was then given a hero's burial, with Adolf Hitler playing a major part in the proceedings.

THE WARTIME SPARING OF AACHEN

Les oz des piedz & des main enserrés,

Par bruit maison long temps inhabitee:

Seront par songes concavant deterrés,

Maison salubre & sans bruyt habitee.

The bones of the feet and the hand are contained

For a long time, thanks to the noise, the house remains uninhabited

They are disinterred by hollow dreams

The healthy and peaceful house is inhabited once again.

The Emperor Charlemagne (742–814), founding father of both France and Germany, and considered by many to be the father of Europe, established Aachen (Aix-La-Chapelle) as his *Roma Secunda* ('second Rome'), intending it to form the major part of his *renovatio imperii Romanorum* ('revival of the Roman Empire') project. In consequence, the imperial palace at Aachen was built on a grandiose scale, and was designed to attract artists, musicians, theologians, scholars and poets to the court of this great Frankish king – one of Jean de Longuyon's 'nine worthies' or 'perfect warriors', alongside Hector, Alexander the Great, Julius Caesar, Joshua, David, Judas Maccabaeus, King Arthur and Godfrey of Bouillon – in an extraordinarily enlightened effort to create a comparativist Court School where all the liberal arts (*artes liberales*) would be taught and later disseminated to a wider world. The original Church of Our Lady (of which the famous Octagon still stands, to this day forming the central core of the remaining sequence of buildings), was without doubt the most magnificent stone edifice north of the Alps at that time.

If you leave the cathedral today, walk to the end of the street and turn immediately right, you will come to the great treasury of Aachen Cathedral, in which lie the famous 'relics' which Nostradamus mentions in line one. One of the primary relics (the mortal remains of saints, etc., as opposed to objects merely connected with them) is known as the Arm Reliquary, and is constructed in the form of an upraised 'hand' (the hand that held Charlemagne's famous sword *Joyeuse*, or 'joyful', which was buried with its owner) within which the ulna and radius of Charlemagne's right forearm can be clearly seen behind a rock-crystal pane of glass. In addition there are the three small reliquaries of Aachen, which purportedly contain the belt of the Virgin Mary, the belt of Jesus Christ, and the scourge with which Christ was whipped on the way to Calvary, and also the gothic three-tower reliquary, which as well as monstrancing Charlemagne's thighbone, is also said to contain a piece of the nail of the Cross, a splinter of the Cross itself, and a fragment of the Crown of Thorns. During the Middle Ages, at the time of the annual shrine pilgrimages, people would come from all over Europe to see the reliquaries, but later the custom was changed to one viewing in every seven years.

Due to the symbolic importance of Aachen to European sensibilities, it was decided, during the Second World War, that the cathedral would be specifically spared during bombing raids. To this end pathfinders were sent ahead to mark the cathedral precincts, and the (largely British) bombing crews effectively avoided destroying what Nostradamus tellingly calls the 'house' (of Europe). On 21 October 1944 there was a massive German surrender at Aachen, which finally brought the restoration of peace so tellingly described by Nostradamus in line four, ending, once and for all, the 'hollow dreams' of the (at least in Charlemagne's terms) 'pagan' Adolf Hitler.

Summary

An outstanding quatrain which suggests the wartime bombing of Aachen, and the enlightened sparing of the cathedral, tomb, and reliquaries of Charlemagne, founding father of Europe.

THE INVASION
OF MONACO

1943

10
3

De sang & faim plus grande calamité
Sept fois s'appreste à la marine plage,
Monech de faim, lieu prins, captivité,
Le grand mené croc en ferrée caige.

An even greater calamity of blood and hunger

Seven times it prepares itself on the strand

Monaco is hungry, captured, taken

The great one hooked up in an iron cage.

We'll have to forget the index date here, because the quatrain clearly refers to the Second World War, and to 'Monaco's' capture in 1943, first by the Italians, under Benito Mussolini, and then under the Nazis, following Mussolini's fall. The Mussolini connection is of particular interest, however, as it is echoed in another quatrain [2/24 – 1945: Adolf Hitler], in which Mussolini's end – he and his mistress were 'hooked up' on the charred frame of a fire-bombed petrol station at Guilino di Mezzegra – is described in a similar fashion: *En caige de fer le grand fera treisner* – 'the great man will find himself paraded inside a cage of iron'.

SUMMARY

The double occupation of Monaco in 1943 – first by the Italians, and then by the Germans.

THE CARPET-BOMBING OF GERMANY & OCCUPIED FRANCE

DATE
1943

NOSTRADAMUS'S INDEX DATE
43

CENTURY NUMBER
5

La grande ruyne des sacrez ne s'esloigne,

Provence, Naples, Secille, seez & Ponce

En Germanie, au Ryn et à Cologne,

Vexés à mort par tous ceulx de Magonce.

The great holy ruin isn't far away

Provence, Naples, Sicily, sees and pontificates

In Germany, on the Rhine and in Cologne

Vexed to death by all those who did not worship fire.

Given that the index date of 43 takes us to the Second World War, '*Magonce*' is the keyword here – it is quite clearly a concatenation of two words, *mage* and *once*. The *mage* were worshippers of fire, and *onc/onques* is an Old French word meaning 'never' – thus 'those who did not worship fire'. The Allies quite clearly fall into this category, as they neither started nor wished for the war, and January 1943 also happens to coincide with the beginning of the carpet-bombing campaign over Germany and occupied France that was to result in the destruction, or partial destruction, of every city and location mentioned in the quatrain.

Summary

The carpet-bombing of Axis-occupied Europe began in January 1943, culminating in the virtual destruction of Old Europe.

THE TIDE OF WAR TURNS FOR THE ALLIES

1943

43

3

Gents d'alentour de Tarn, Loth, & Garonne,

Gardés les monts Apennines passer,

Vostre tombeau pres de Rome & d'Anconne

Le noir poil crespe fera trophée dresser.

People from around the Tarn, the Lot,
the Garonne

And the Gard pass the Apennine mountains

Your tomb near Rome and Ancona

The black frizzy-haired one will raise up a pageant.

The year 1943 saw the tide turn against the Axis powers. 'Rome' was bombed for the first time on 19 July, and the railway line from 'Ancona' to Pescara was destroyed by the SAS that same October ('your tomb near Rome and Ancona').

Emperor Haile Selassie ('the black frizzy-haired one') could finally be confident that Ethiopia would not suffer reinvasion by the Italians, following Italy's declaration of war against Germany on 13 October. And at the Teheran Conference, held from 28 November to 3 December, the Tripartite Powers formally began discussing the invasion of France ('People from around the Tarn, the Lot, the Garonne, and the Gard pass the Apennine mountains').

SUMMARY

A wide-ranging and accurate quatrain detailing events during the latter part of 1943, when the tide of war finally began to turn in the Allies' favour.

RIVIERA D-DAY

5 AUGUST 1944

23

10

Au peuple ingrat faictes les remonstrances,

Par lors l'armee se saisira d'Antibe,

Dans l'arc Monech feront les doleances,

Et à Frejus l'un l'autre prendra ribe.

Reproofs are made to the ungrateful people

And then the army seizes Antibes

They will grieve in the gulf of Monaco

And at Fréjus the windmill will change hands.

The Aurelian Way was one of the most important Roman roads in Europe, and ran from Rome to Arles, taking in 'Monaco', 'Antibes', and 'Fréjus'. Given the index date of 23, linking the three towns mentioned in a period outside the Roman era should have been easy – for they are, after all, not very far apart – but the reality proved somewhat different. Finally, the quatrain must be deemed unsatisfactorily Napoleonic, in the sense that Napoleon was imprisoned for two weeks in the Chateau d'Antibes following the fall of the elder Robespierre – but that was in 1794, just after his success at ejecting the British from Toulon. An alternative reading would link the quatrain to the Riviera D-Day in 1944.

SUMMARY

An unsatisfactory quatrain that could apply either to Napoleon, or to the Riviera D-Day of 5 August 1944, which saw American parachutists landing near Fréjus, and 60,000 troops disembarking between Cavalaire and Agay, just 20 miles to the west of Antibes.

POPE PIUS XII

1944

44
5

Par mer le rouge sera prins de pirates,

La paix sera par son moyen troublée:

L'ire & l'avare commettra par fainct acte,

Au grand Pontife sera l'armee doublee.

The red one is at sea and will be taken by pirates

His action disturbs the peace

Anger and greed ensue through a refusal to act

The army will be overtaken by the great Pontiff.

Rome was liberated on 4 and 5 June 1944, and on 8 June Pope Pius XII held an audience for the victorious Allied army, which he conducted in seven languages. The 'refusal to act' could apply to the pope's lukewarm response to the enforced deportation of Roman and Hungarian Jews, although political expedience, and the intervention of the Red Cross and the King of Sweden (together with the Allies), ensured an end to the deportations on 8 July.

SUMMARY

A tentative quatrain, which appears to apply to Pope Pius XII ('the red one' – i.e. leader of the red-frocked cardinals; 'red' was also the devil's colour in medieval France), and his actions during the course of 1944, a crucial year in the Allied struggle against Germany.

THE SIEGE OF CALAIS

1944

45
8

La main escharpe & la iambe bandee,

Longs puis nay de Calais portera,

Au mot du guet la mort sera tardee,

Puis dans le temple à Pasque saignera.

With his hand slashed and his leg bound up

Lengthwise the youngest son is carried to Calais

His death is delayed by the password

Later he will bleed in the temple at Easter.

There is an almost religious aspect to this quatrain, as it was Jesus Christ who 'bled in the temple at Easter', when he was scourged before being taken off to be crucified. Given the index date of 45, it is more than likely that this quatrain refers to the Second World War, and to the liberation of 'Calais' on 30 September 1944, after a seven-day siege – this carries echoes of the siege of Calais by King Edward III of England, almost exactly 600 years earlier, in August 1347.

The identity of the injured 'youngest son' remains something of a mystery, although Froissart's *Chronicles* (which spans the period 1322–1400, incorporating the medieval siege of Calais) contains a long section about the duel between Lord de Chary and Sir Piers Courteney, whom de Chary was escorting back to Calais after the completion of a formal joust before the king in Paris. The two men set up their own private tournament just outside the town, which resulted in Sir Piers being lanced in the shoulder – he was later carried back to Calais by his friends, and de Chary was flung temporarily in jail as a punishment for harming a man under the protection of the king of France.

SUMMARY

This quatrain describes the siege of Calais in 1944, by the Czechs and the Canadians, and the wounding of an unnamed combatant – a story that Nostradamus may have borrowed from the Froissart *Chronicles*.

ADOLF HITLER

Bestes farouches de faim fluves tranner:

Plus part du camp encontre Hister sera,

En caige de fer le grand sera treisner,

Quand Rin enfant Germain observera.

With the hunger of wild beasts they will cross
the rivers

Most of the country will be against Hister

The great man will find himself paraded inside
a cage of iron

The German child [of the Rhine] will see nothing.

An understandably famous quatrain which appears to link the word 'Hister' (Hitler/Danube) with 'German', and which delineates, in line three, the fate of Adolf Hitler's chief ally, Benito Mussolini, whose manner of death is accurately described as being 'paraded inside a cage of iron' (following the shooting of Mussolini and his mistress, Clara Petacci, in Guilino di Mezzegra, near Lake Como, Italy, their bodies were taken back to Milan and hung on meat hooks in the charred metal frame of a fire-bombed petrol station in the Piazzale Loreto). '*Hister*' has a further link to Hitler, however, beyond the euphonic, for it was the Latin name for the Danube River – Hitler was born on a tributary of the Danube (Braunau am Inn) and grew up on its banks, in Linz. Nostradamus uses the word *Hister* again in 5/29 – 1629: Shah Abbas the Great II, and 4/68 – 1768: The Travails of Pope Clement XIII (both prophecies can be found in my *The Complete Prophecies of Nostradamus*), but on both these subsequent occasions purely in the sense of the Danube.

Line one takes the river symbolism even further, however, for it clearly refers to the Russian army, which crossed the Elbe and the Vistula rivers in 1945 ('they will cross the rivers'), as part of their push into Germany, before raping 'like wild beasts' many tens of thousands of German women, in a coldly premeditated revenge for the horrors of Stalingrad.

The last line is a particularly haunting one, as it appears to echo the reiterated statement made by millions of Germans after the war that they had no knowledge of Hitler's so-called Final Solution ('the German child sees nothing').

SUMMARY

A wonderful quatrain, which twins the four 'rivers' of the Rhine, the Danube, the Elbe, and the Vistula, with those who both cross, and are of them. The quatrain brings together Adolf Hitler, Benito Mussolini, and Germany's eventual nemesis, the embittered and brutalized Russian army, in a clear depiction of the final catastrophic year of the Second World War.

THE DOWNFALL
OF THE THIRD REICH

1945

45
5

Le grand Empire sera tost désolé,

Et translaté pres d'arduer ne silve

Les deux bastardz par l'aisné decollé,

Et regnera Aenobarbe, nay de milve.

The great Empire will be completely devastated

And transformed near the Ardennes into
disparate pieces

The two spurious ones will be beheaded by
their senior

Aenobarbus, the kite-born [hawk-nosed] one,
will reign.

The Latin word for the Ardennes Forest was '*Ardvenna Silva*' (*see* line two in the French), which is the likely meaning of what may well be a typographical error (it was rectified in later editions of *The Centuries*). However *ardu* is also an Old French adjective meaning arduous, *ne* means not, and *silves*, as well as meaning the same as *silva*, a wood, can also means a collection of disparate pieces (such as were collected together by the later Latin poets) – and we know how Nostradamus likes his puns and his wordplays!

With all that said, this quatrain is clearly about the destruction of the Third Reich in 1945 ('the great Empire will be completely devastated'), following the failure of von Rundstedt's deadly 'Ardennes' campaign of 16 December 1944 to 25 January 1945. The 'two spurious ones' are Hitler and Mussolini, both of whom were to die within two days of each other, and barely three months after the events mentioned here. Aenobarbus means 'the bronze-bearded one', and refers to the magical 'translation' by Castor and Pollux (the Dioscuri) of a formerly black beard into bronze after the Battle of Lake Regullus – the ancient Aenobarbus family of Rome (to whom the legend applied) was described by Suetonius as having a trans-generational 'vicious streak', and the orator Licinius Crassus remarked of one member:

> Should his bronze beard really surprise us?
> After all, the man has a face of iron and a heart made of lead.

One wonders whether the 'kite-born/hawk-nosed' man who will reign after the destruction of Germany in 1945 is not Stalin – the 'steel man', whom Crassus described as 'the man with a face of iron'? Either way this is a brilliant quatrain, index-date perfect and geographically exact.

PART THREE

THE THIRD ANTICHRIST: 'THE ONE STILL TO COME'

NOSTRADAMUS'S 'THIRD ANTICHRIST' QUATRAINS CONCATENATED

Now, having got the 19th and 20th centuries and all their associated disasters out of the way – and to further reinforce the very real threat of what Nostradamus tells us is likely to occur during the course of the 21st century – I am going to do something which has never been done before. I am going to concatenate my English translation of all of Nostradamus's Third Antichrist quatrains into one continuous narrative (I would refer you to my chapter entitled 'The Third Antichrist: The One Still to Come', for my line by line commentary on the poem).

I think my readers will agree, when they read the following, that it makes for a truly stunning dramatic narrative:

Stained with mass murder and adultery
This great enemy of humanity
Will be worse than any man before him
In steel, fire, water, bloody and monstrous
Though born in poverty, he will take supreme power

He will tyrannize and bankrupt his people

Raising a thousand-year army

He will seem lucky, though he costs both lives
and money

Milk and the blood of frogs flows in Dalmatia

Battle is joined, there is plague near Balennes

Wailing will echo throughout enslaved Slovenia

When the monster is born in and near Ravenna

At the total eclipse of the sun

The monster will be seen in broad daylight

He will be misinterpreted

None will have foreseen the great cost

From deep in the Western part of Europe

A child will be born, to poor parents

He will seduce the multitude with his tongue

The noise of his reputation will grow in the Eastern
kingdom

A great King falls into the hands of a youngster

There is confusion around Easter time, and a knife-
blow

Long-term captives, and St Elmo's Fire

At a time when three brothers wound and kill
each other

The young Nero, using three chimneys

Will burn the living word in his ardour

Happy the person far from such practices

Three of his own blood will watch him die

Mabus, though dead, returns

Both man and beast suffer terribly

Then, all of a sudden, vengeance arrives

Much blood, thirst, hunger, when the comet passes

With the plague over, the earth shrinks

Peace will reign for a good while

People will travel through the sky, like birds, and by
    sea and wave

Before war once again is called for

London's prime minister, ruled by America

Will freeze out the Scottish enclave

The Rob Roys will pick themselves so false an
    Antichrist

That they will all be thrown into the mix

The shining deed of the newly elected elder

Will be blown south by the great northern wind

Great halls are raised by his own sweat

Fleeing, he is killed at the bushes of Ambellon

The great mountain, seven stades around

After peace, war, hunger, flood

Will roll far, destroying great swathes of country

Even antiquities, and mighty foundations

From the regions governed by Libra

A great war will come, enough to disturb the
    mountains

Both sexes will be captured, and all Byzantium

So that cries will be heard at dawn, from country to
country

Slicing armour is hidden in the torches

Inside Lyon, on the day of the sacred mountain

Those of Vienna will be put in the mincer

By the Latin cantons; Macon does not lie

The spear from the skies will complete its
extinguishing

It will speak of death: a terrible execution

The proud nation will be returned to the stone
in the tree

Rumours of a human, brutish monster bring first
catharsis, then sacrifice

He will enter, ugly, bad, and infamous

He will tyrannize Mesopotamia

Friends will pretend that the adulterous one
has a soul

The land is horrible, and black of aspect

The islanders will face a long siege

They will defend themselves vigorously

Those outside will be assailed by hunger

It will be a far worse famine than those which
preceded it

The cry of an extraordinary bird will be heard

Cannoning through the air shafts

The cost of a bushel of wheat corn will soar so high

That man will make of man a cannibal

The eagerly awaited one will never return

To Europe, but will reappear in Asia

One of the confederacy descended from great
Hermes

He will grow above all other kings of the Orient

The Third Antichrist will soon be annihilated

His war will have lasted for twenty-seven years

The heretics are either dead, captive, or exiled

Human blood reddens the water that covers the
earth in hail

By arcs of fire, pitch, and flame are they repulsed

Screams, cries, and shouts at midnight

They are launched from inside the smashed
defences

The traitors escape through their secret passages

Sudden joy inside sudden sadness

Will occur at Rome, of the jealously guarded
favours

Mourning, cries, tears, weeping, blood, excellent joy

Opposing groups surprised and locked up

The locked and fated eternal order of things

Will switch direction, thanks to a new order

The old Greek order will be broken

Its citadel taken; the enemy will not be accepted

The blood of innocents, of widows and virgins

The great Red One commits many evils

Holy images are infused with the light of votive
candles

Terrified and fearful, people will no longer dare to
move

Near the great river a ditch will form; the land will
be eaten

The water will split into fifteen channels

The city falls; fire, blood, and cries conflict

Much of it caused by the collision

The royal bird will fly over the city of the sun

Seven months earlier there will be a nocturnal augury

The Eastern wall will fall, amidst thunder and
lightning

For seven unremitting days the enemy will be
at the gates

The great scolder, bold and shameless

Will be elected head of the army

The boldness of his contentions

Will cause the bridge to break and the city to faint
with fear

When even the trees shake mightily

And the south wind seems covered in blood

So many will try to escape

That Vienna and all Austria will shake with their
passing

Fréjus, Antibes, and the towns around Nice

Will be devastated both by land and by sea

Locusts will come on propitious winds

Kidnap, death, rape, pillage, no martial law

When the sun is at 20° in Taurus, a great
earthquake

Will totally destroy the packed Great Theatre

Air, sky, and earth will be murky and unsettled

So that even Infidels will call on God and the saints
to steer them

He will be born of the pit and of the
immeasurable city

Product of dark and infernal parents

Who wish the power of the great and revered king

To be destroyed by Rouen and Evreux

The old demagogue, with the salt measure teetering

Will be urged never to release the captive

The old man, though not weak, does not wish to be
maligned

By legitimate means he delivers him to his friends

It will seem to human beings that the gods

Must have been the authors of the great war

Once, long ago, the sky was clear of weapons

Whereas now, on the left hand, there is damage still
to come.

Formerly inhabited lands will become unfit for
human life

Cultivatable fields will be divided up

Power will be given to overcautious fools

From that moment on, death and discord for the great brothers

New laws will rule new lands

Towards Syria, Judea and Palestine

The great barbarian empire will decay

Before Phoebus concludes his dominance of the century

Time present and time past

Will be judged by the great comedian

The world will tire of him when it is too late

Having forsaken its conventional clergy

When the great number seven completes itself

Games will begin at the Tomb side

Not far from the turn of the Millennium

The dead will rise out of their graves.

After Nostradamus's extraordinarily accurate depictions of the first two Antichrists, Napoleon Bonaparte and Adolf Hitler, in 47 and 30 quatrains respectively, his rendition of the Third Antichrist, in a further 36 quatrains, becomes even more sinister.

This is a man, we are told, who will, like both of his predecessors, start a global rather than simply a pan-European war, on a scale, however, unsurpassed by even the First or Second World Wars. In addition, there will be both a run-up and an aftermath to this catastrophic conflict which will, quite literally, change the face of the earth.

If you look carefully at the chapter I have entitled 'Nostradamus's 'Third Antichrist' Quatrains Concatenated', in which I have run together all of Nostradamus's original verses dealing with the Antichrist into one continuous narrative poem, a number of potential secrets are revealed. For a start, the true nature of the Beast is clearly delineated.

I will now go through the poem line by line for you, picking out particular elements and key lines that I think might throw light on the character and significance to humanity of the 'One Still to Come'.

The first line of Nostradamus's – I shall call it the Concatenation from here on in, for ease of reference – introduces him clearly. He will be both a 'mass murderer' and an 'adulterer'. It is important to remember here that adultery/adulteration does not simply imply uxorial betrayal. It is also an alchemical term. And Nostradamus is almost certainly using it in that sense, implying someone who adulterates, or dilutes – i.e. a man who weakens, changes, and transforms things. The person concerned is also 'the great enemy of humanity' – in other words he is everyone's enemy, and will eventually bring down even those who blindly follow him (just as Hitler and Napoleon did with their followers).

As with Jesus – whose evil mirror image he is – the Third Antichrist will be 'born in poverty'. This conceivably affords him kudos, and allows him to gather to himself the poor and dispossessed of the world, who wrongly believe that he is one of them – just as they felt that Hitler was one of them (he ended the Great War a lance corporal, or in US terms a private first class – even his name means 'one who lives in a hut'), and that Napoleon was one of them, because he, too, began his career at the bottom (even though he was born into the minor gentry, and benefited accordingly, both financially and in terms of status).

'He will seem lucky' – think of both Hitler and Napoleon's early campaigns. Both of them appeared to have the luck of the damned, with Hitler, in particular, benefiting from his arrogation of the – originally Russian – concept of the Blitzkrieg. This seeming 'luck' tempted people into the Antichristian camp who would not otherwise have considered coming over – the world has always valued a 'lucky' man, believing, perhaps, that the condition is catching.

'He will be misinterpreted', meaning that, again as with Adolf Hitler, otherwise well-meaning people will falsely judge the Third Antichrist to be a good man (many thousands of otherwise sane German women believed that Hitler would have made the ideal husband, and wrote to him accordingly, often enclosing their house keys).

He will 'burn the living word in his ardour' – all tyrants, from Julius Caesar (who inadvertently burned the Great

Brucheum Library when he set fire to the fleet in Alexandria Harbour), through Bishop de Landa in the Yucatan (who burned the Maya Codices), and Adolf Hitler, via Josef Goebbels, and via some particularly gullible students, who burned 25,000 allegedly un-German books in Berlin, on 10 May 1933, as part of a nationwide move to reaffirm traditional values – have seen fit, at some point or another, either to burn the books of those who disagreed with them, or otherwise censor free speech. Heinrich Heine, the great German poet and humanist, wrote in his *Almansor* in 1821, '*Dort, wo man Bücher verbrennt, verbrennt Mann am ende auch Menschen*' – 'wherever people burn books, there, finally, they will also burn people.'

'Mabus, though dead, returns' – this is another dark echo of the reincarnation of Jesus Christ (of whom the Third Antichrist is the evil mirror image). *Abus*, in French, means abuse or misuse, and *je m'abuse* means 'I abuse myself' – while *maboul* which has euphonic connections to *mabus*, means a lunatic or a crackpot.

There will even be a period of false peace ('peace will reign for a good while'), just as there was in Adolf Hitler's time, following British Prime Minister Neville Chamberlain's now infamous 'peace in our time' speech after the trumped-up and misconceived Munich Agreement of 30 September 1938. And just as there was in Napoleonic Europe after the 27 March 1802 Treaty of Amiens, which ushered in a curious one-year period in which tourism restarted, and genteel English ladies and their husbands were able, once again, to visit their Paris couturiers – hostilities, somewhat inevitably, given the benefit of hindsight, restarted on 16 May 1803.

The coming Great War ('enough to disturb mountains'),

and triggered by the Third Antichrist, will be prefaced by a series of events, including the striking of the earth by a comet ('the great mountain, seven stades around... will roll far, destroying great swathes of country'), and the death of a 'newly elected leader' at 'the bushes of Ambellon'. Ambellon, in this case, is most probably an anagram of Bellona, the ancient Roman goddess of war (*bellum*, in Latin, means war), whose priests used to split open their thighs and use the blood in their 'predictive' rites.

'Rumours of a human, brutish monster bring first catharsis, then sacrifice' – this is a fascinating conceit, as, traditionally, catharsis (a.k.a. purging or purification) follows sacrifice (a.k.a. evacuation, according to Aristotle), surely? Or as Walter Burkert puts it, in his *The Orientalizing Revolution*, in Greek cathartic practice 'blood is purified through blood... a piglet must be slaughtered in such a way that its blood pours over the polluted man; the blood is then washed off...', just as was done by Apollo at Troezene in the case of Orestes (who had, with some justification, murdered his mother, Clytemnestra), leading to renewal, and the washing away of guilt (Orestes died happily of old age, in his 90th year). But what if the system is reversed? Surely, then, the guilt is not washed away, but simply reinforced?

'Friends will pretend that the adulterous one has a soul'. This is a clear harking back to the first line of the Concatenation, and echoes the wish-fulfilment fantasies present in so many erstwhile allies of both Hitler and Napoleon, who managed to convince themselves, despite all appearances to the contrary, that the men to whose wall they had nailed their colours might not be the murderous rogues they belatedly suspected them to be.

A 'famine' follows, and the 'cry of an extraordinary bird' is heard 'cannoning through the air shafts'. Could this be the roc, a fabulous white bird of an unbelievable size, which was allegedly able to truss elephants in its talons and carry them back to its nest according to the Arabian Nights? Or might it be the phoenix, another fabulous bird, which, upon living a certain number of years, makes itself a pyre of spices, sings a final dirge ('the cry of an extraordinary bird') and immolates itself, only to reappear again in order to repeat its life exactly as before (remember, five paragraphs back, 'Mabus, though dead, returns').

Nostradamus's image in line 73 of the Concatenation, 'that man will make of man a cannibal', seems clear enough – Cormac McCarthy, for instance, uses it brilliantly in his End-of-the-World/Armageddon novel *The Road*). But I believe, also, that Nostradamus meant it to be taken metaphorically, in the sense, let's say, of the suicide bomber, destroying both himself *and* his victims in what he believes, erroneously, to be justifiable murder.

Then we are back to Nostradamus's beloved number 'seven' again (*see* the beginning of my chapter entitled 'Nostradamus's Antichrists' for my riff on the significance the number seven might have had for the seer). 'Seven months earlier there will be a nocturnal augury' – 'for seven unremitting days the enemy will be at the gates' – 'when the great number seven completes itself, games will begin at the Tomb side.' Seven, in this context, clearly represents a summing up – and end, if you like, of holiness, or the holy time.

For in the final analysis Nostradamus clearly believed that his powers of prediction only encompassed, in detail, a period of roughly 700 years, from the 15th to the 21st century. It is also clear, however, that he does not feel that the antics of the man he calls the Third Antichrist will result in what eschatologists call 'the End of the World' or 'Armageddon'. This will occur, according to Nostradamus, roughly 7,000 years after the birth of Jesus Christ, and will involve a Final Judgement by one he calls 'the Great Comedian'.

So what Nostradamus appears to be describing in his 36 Third Antichrist quatrains is less a holocaust than a virtual repositioning of the world *before* Armageddon occurs – a final twisting on its axis of a world which will have a further 5,000 years to go after the appearance of the Third Antichrist, and in which to digest the lessons it has learned from his effect. Does this mean that there are further Antichrists to come? Who can say. Nostradamus, certainly, does not choose to delineate them.

Nostradamus's great closing image, in the final line of the Concatenation, that 'the dead will rise out of their graves', however, is a clear reference to the Eastern Orthodox tradition of the Doom painting (the Last Judgement), of which perhaps the greatest of all examples is still visible on the westernmost outside wall of the sacred Monastery of Voronet, at Suceava, Romania. It was actually painted during Nostradamus's lifetime (circa 1547 – Nostradamus lived from 1503-66), under the aegis of Archbishop Grigore Rosca.

The mural, which I visited and photographed in 2009, is designed in five horizontal registers, with 'the whole scene crossed, like the diagonal line of a trapezium, by the river of the fire of Hell'. In the lower right-hand corner, in a scene entitled *The Resurrection of the Dead at the Last Judgement*, we clearly see the dead, in twos, man and woman, rising out of their communal graves, just as Nostradamus describes in his final quatrain. They are dressed in white grave garments (possibly suggesting a return to the innocence of birth/rebirth), and they are clearly responding to the call of an angel's trumpet.

But here is the ultimate curiosity. The dead are accompanied on their journey by certain symbolical animals – a dog, a fox, a bear, a lion, a dragon, a snake, a wolf, and a wild boar – each carrying a human heart in their mouth, intent on giving back to God the souls they have devoured during their lifetimes.

Only a deer has nothing in her mouth, as she, being non-carnivorous, is deemed entirely innocent, having nothing whatsoever to release.

THE THIRD ANTICHRIST'S ASTROLOGICAL CHART

Bearing in mind all that we know, thanks to Nostradamus, about the possible details of the Third Antichrist's conception and birth, we are now able to extrapolate, with a fair degree of accuracy, what his astrological chart might be. We know, for instance, thanks to quatrain 3/34 – 2034: Birth of the Third Antichrist – Presage III, that the Third Antichrist will be conceived in the period immediately following the total solar eclipse of 20 March 2034 – an eclipse that will pass over Central Africa, the Middle East (including Egypt and Iran), and South Asia (including India and China) – and that he will be born in the New Year of 2035. We also know that he will be born inside a triangle roughly incorporating Ravenna in Italy, Ravna Reka in Serbia, and Ravne na Koroskem in Slovenia. If we look at this triangle, we see that the obvious central point, in terms of an acceptable average, is Banja Luka in Bosnia and Herzegovina (scene of some of the worst of the ethnic cleansing during the Bosnian war, which included the destruction of 16 mosques by Radovan Karadzic's Serb authorities). I shall use Banja Luka, therefore, for want of a better, as the geographical location and anchor of the Third Antichrist's astrological chart.

Let's assume for a moment, then, that his conception occurs on or around 21 March. The World Health Organization allows for between 37 and 42 weeks of gestation for a normal pregnancy, with the average time for parturition occurring 40 weeks after the last menstrual period (assuming, for a moment, that the mother concerned has a normal 28 day regular cycle). In other words childbirth occurs an average of 38 weeks after actual conception. That's 266 days.

But we know this does not occur in the case of the Third Antichrist, because Nostradamus places his birth in 2035. So let's assume the Third Antichrist is born on New Year's Day – a date which would seem to be both symbolically and ironically accurate. That would give a 286-day parturition, from a conception date of 21 March, which seems a little high. Deduct 10 or 11 days, let's say, for the end of the last menstrual cycle, and we are suddenly dead on the button at 275 days, and a birth date of 1 January 2035, giving us a little over 39 weeks of parturition. A normal, natural term baby, then.

The following is what we get if we figure the Third Antichrist's notional birth date as 1 January (i.e. New Year's Day) 2035, at a little after midnight, in the central geographical location of Banja Luka in Bosnia and Herzegovina. And Readers, please bear in mind that this is an entirely theoretical exercise.

THE THIRD ANTICHRIST'S
BIRTH CHART

Born: Monday 1 January 2035
Time: 00.05 (CET -1.00)
Place: Banja Luka, Bosnia and Herzegovina
Location: 44N46 17E11

Planetary Placements

Sun in Capricorn

Ascendant in Libra

Moon in Libra

Mercury in Capricorn

Venus in Scorpio

Mars in Scorpio

Jupiter in Aries

Saturn in Leo

Uranus in Cancer

Neptune in Aries

Pluto in Aquarius

Midheaven in Cancer

North Node in Virgo

Planetary Aspects

Sun: Square challenging Moon
Sun: Square challenging Jupiter
Sun: Opposition confronting Uranus
Sun: Square challenging Ascendant
Sun: Opposition confronting Midheaven
Moon: Opposition confronting Jupiter
Moon: Sextile cooperating with Saturn
Moon: Square challenging Uranus
Moon: Conjunct uniting with Ascendant
Mercury: Sextile cooperating with Venus
Mercury: Sextile cooperating with Mars
Mercury: Opposition confronting Saturn
Mercury: Square challenging Neptune
Venus: Conjunct uniting with Mars
Venus: Square challenging Pluto
Mars: Square challenging Pluto
Jupiter: Trine harmonizing with Saturn
Jupiter: Square challenging Uranus
Jupiter: Opposition confronting Ascendant
Uranus: Square challenging Ascendant
Uranus: Conjunct uniting with Midheaven
Neptune: Sextile cooperating with Pluto
Pluto: Trine harmonizing with Ascendant

Astrological Summary

This is a man who likes being alone. He is disciplined, practical and prudent. But also, at times, both miserly and grudging – something that may be exacerbated by his Libran ascendant, which will exaggerate his disinclination towards self-criticism, increase his self-satisfaction, and aggravate his refusal to acknowledge anything in the way of personal flaws (Adolf Hitler, too, had a Libran ascendant).

The Third Antichrist will be jealous of his prerogatives – he will not tolerate anything that smacks of disloyalty. The material world will matter more to him than the world of emotions. He will wish to exercise control over everything he touches – there will be little or no delegation with this man. He will aim for the top and wish to stay there. He will be fundamentally unsure of himself, and he will disguise this with a false self-confidence. It will be lonely at the top, but this individual will refuse to show either weakness or vulnerability, and will thus isolate himself entirely from any conceivable influence for good in his life. He will not use mentors. He will not take advice. He will not listen.

The Third Antichrist's Moon is also in Libra, which will, on the surface, allow the Antichrist to seem diplomatic – a peacemaker, even. But his underlying aggression will show through when all does not go his way, and he may be subject to great rages if he feels he has been unfairly dealt with.

The Third Antichrist's Mercury in Capricorn, twinned with his Sun sign in Capricorn, make him easily capable of getting rid of any perceived rivals. This is a calculating and thoughtful man, who carefully judges what will most work to his advantage.

The Third Antichrist's Venus in Scorpio may make of him

a voluptuary, too, further emphasizing Nostradamus's use of the word 'adultery', in line 1 of the Concatenation. He will have problems expressing what he feels for others, and may simply abuse them sexually, or use them as objects (think of Mussolini, Stalin, and Mao Zedong, all of whom abused their positions of power and privilege in search of sexual gratification). His Mars – equally in Scorpio – may exacerbate this tendency, further reinforcing the possessive nature of the Beast, and his voluptuary aspect. He will also be likely to attempt to compensate for his emotional shortcomings via obsessive secrecy.

Jupiter in Aries will simply add to the Third Antichrist's disregard of possible consequences. This placement suits people who don't give a damn for the effects of their actions on other people. In the worst scenario (readers will forgive me if I tend towards the negative here!) such people can be boastful and vainglorious, constantly blowing their own trumpet and overwhelming others with the scale of their purported achievements. Saturn in Leo merely exacerbates the autocratic nature of the Beast, and makes him less likely to see things as they really are, but rather as he wishes them to be.

He will be proud and unswerving, and will show a marked refusal to accept any limitations on his behaviour whatsoever. When he reaches the pinnacle of his ambitions, this man will still not be satisfied, and will force issues ever further, until there is no possibility of a return of the status quo. Perspectives are lost, judgement is flawed, and loyalty by others goes unrewarded. Such a man is authoritarian to an extreme degree, and can appear immutably austere once bedecked with total power.

Uranus in Cancer reinforces the idiosyncratic nature of the

Beast. He will be moody, and changeable, and prone to violent emotional swings, to the extent that underlings may be confused as to his real wishes. This then harks back to his Sun sign of Capricorn, which in its negative aspects can lead to the inhibitions and to the lack of self-confidence which may lie behind such intemperate behaviour.

And yes, with Cancer as his Midheaven, twinned with a rising Libra, worry will eat away even further at this man's self-confidence, making of him a potentially very dangerous human being indeed.

THE THIRD ANTICHRIST TIMELINE

2010: Nostradamus warns us that the Third Antichrist will be even more destructive than his two predecessors. His actions will darken and distort the history of the 21st century.

2032: The Third Antichrist will soon be born. His birth will be a disaster for the world.

Three possible sites for the birth of the Third Antichrist are given – he will born near Ravenna, Italy, or possibly near Ravna Reka, in Serbia, or Ravne na Koroskem, in Slovenia. Those countries abutting the place of his birth should fear the future.

2034: The total eclipse on 20 March will presage the Third Antichrist's birth – he will be conceived in the period immediately following the eclipse, and born in the New Year.

2035: The Third Antichrist is born of poor parents. Nostradamus predicts that his birth will lead to global warfare and ecological damage on an unprecedented scale.

2036: Certain parties will declare the Third Antichrist to be the Second Coming. This suggestion will damage both the Christian Church and the world community.

2053: The Third Antichrist starts to build his power base. There is extreme censorship. Nostradamus compares the Antichrist to the young Nero.

2062: There is a worldwide epidemic, allowing the Antichrist to consolidate his power with the disenchanted. Nostradamus coins the name Mabus.

2063: Following the horror of the epidemic, there is a brief hiatus, in which the world is nominally at peace. This allows the Third Antichrist to marshal his forces, just as Hitler marshalled his during the period of appeasement.

2066: Nostradamus brings us the smaller picture, too. A misguided Scotland is taken in by the force of the Antichrist's oratory, allying itself with the powers of darkness against England.

2069: There are rumbles of a future global war, despite the efforts of a new leader of the free world.

An asteroid strikes the earth, causing immense damage. Is this a foretaste of things to come?

2070: The Global War begins, triggered by the Islamic world.

The Third Antichrist, now aged 35, has achieved his principal objective when thermonuclear devices are used on the battlefield.

The war is brutal and swift. Unparalleled destruction has been rained upon the earth. The Third Antichrist makes his move.

He attempts to benefit from the post-nuclear fallout. People in search of a leader are drawn to him. He makes his new base in the Middle East.

2071: England has somehow contrived to hold itself aloof from the conflict. It becomes the potential bread basket of a ruined Europe, but only has enough to feed its own people.

2075: It is the end of a great human era. All is changing. The world is entering a period of barbarism and uncertainty.

The Third Antichrist has survived the global war of 2070. Now, at the age of only 40, he is attempting to widen his sphere of influence from the Middle East into Asia.

2077: The Third Antichrist is not having everything his own way. For the first time it seems that he may be fallible. People rise up against him. Blood covers the earth.

Britain attempts to seal its borders. Fifth columnists attempt to undermine its attempts to remain outside the fray, but they fail.

2078: Totalitarian government abounds. Any attempt at democratic change is ruthlessly put down.

2079: There is a fundamental change in the world order. Democratic forces attempt, like the Phocenes, a last-ditch resistance and are, to everyone's surprise, successful.

2080: There is vast ongoing ecological change, thanks to the thermonuclear war of ten years before. People turn back to God in their horror at what has been allowed to occur.

The toe of Italy is devastated by a tsunami, triggered by an underwater volcano.

A further tsunami devastates the Aegean area, including parts of Turkey.

2081: A new leader appears, and attempts to turn back the clock. People flock to him.

2082: The ecological destruction, triggered by the 2070 thermonuclear war, continues, this time with a catastrophic earthquake. Its epicentre will be somewhere near the border between the Czech Republic and Austria.

There are locust plagues in Europe. The locusts are carried over from Africa by freak winds.

2083: A terrible earthquake hits New York. Its effect will be far greater than the 9/11 tragedy, to which this quatrain bears a strong resemblance.

2084: Nostradamus sums up the effect the Third Antichrist has had on the earth.

2085: Is the Third Antichrist captured? Either way, the French leader who holds him captive is weak and havering. He is given back into the hands of his allies.

2091: It is 20 years after the end of the Global War of 2070/71. People and nations are slowly coming together in their desire to start afresh. Further conflict is feared, however.

2095: There is ecological burn-out. Great swathes of the world are uninhabitable. There is still no effective leadership in the world.

2097: The Antichrist's influence has waned. 'New laws rule new lands'. Nostradamus likens the decay of the Third Antichrist's empire to that of the Holy Roman Emperor Charles V, who was destined to sit inside the Wunderberg, with all his knights and vassals around him, until his grey beard was long enough to encircle the table three times – following which the Antichrist would reappear.

7073: Nostradamus likens the world's end to a joke by the 'Great Comedian'. He imagines Satan, or the final Antichrist, cutting a caper at the side of mankind's universal tomb.

7074: The Final Prophecy. It is the time of Armageddon. The joke is on us. The 'Great Comedian' has won. All that mankind thought would last has turned into dust.

THE THIRD
ANTICHRIST
QUATRAINS

ADVANCE WARNING OF THIRD ANTICHRIST

Tasche de murdre enormes adulteres,

Grand ennemy de tout le genre humain

Que sera pire qu'ayeulx, oncles, ne peres

En fer, feu, eau, sanguin & inhumain.

Stained with mass murder and adultery

This great enemy of humanity

Will be worse than any man before him

In steel, fire, water, bloody and monstrous.

This is an early portent of the coming of the Third Antichrist, echoing the warning tones of St John The Evangelist in I John 2. xvii–xviii, even down to St John's concept of the transitory lust for material things, as postulated in 'And the world passeth away, and the lust thereof'. Nostradamus certainly doesn't pull any punches here, describing the future depredations of the Antichrist as 'worse than any man before him', which, if one considers the first two Antichrists to be either Napoleon and Hitler, or Stalin and Hitler, depending on which reading one adheres to, is really saying something. Go to 7/32 and 2/32 – 2032, 3/34 – 2034, 3/35 – 2035, 9/36 – 2036, 10/75 – 2075 and 8/77 – 2077 for a further taste of what lies in store for the next few generations.

SUMMARY

The Third Antichrist will be even more destructive than his two predecessors, and the results of his actions will darken and distort the history of the 21st century.

BIRTH OF THE THIRD ANTICHRIST – PRESAGE I

2032

32

7

Du mont Royal naistra d'une casane,

Qui cave & compte viendra tyranniser,

Dresser copie de la marche Millane,

Favene Florence d'or & gens expuiser.

Though born in poverty, he will take supreme power

He will tyrannize and bankrupt his people

Raising a thousand-year army

He will seem lucky, though he costs both lives and money.

This is a presage to the great quatrain number 3/35 – 2035 [Birth of the Third Antichrist]. Nostradamus often plays these games, referring back to earlier quatrains whose meaning he was unsure of at the time. There is much wordplay in this one, which would allow for two separate readings. However, if we acknowledge the wordplay, and do not take '*Millane*', '*Favene*' and '*Florence*' as literally meaning Milan, Faenza and Florence, we come up with *mille ans* for *Millane* ('a thousand years'), *sa veine* for *Faveine* ('his luck'), and 'gold florins' for *Florence d'or*.

Place names were rarely fixed in Nostradamus, and were often capitalized to draw attention to themselves and to the secrets hidden inside them, as with his use of the word *Hister*, for example, in the famous Hitler quatrains presaging the Second World War (Hitler was the second Antichrist). *Hister*, as well as meaning the Danube, near which Hitler was born, can also mean hysteria, from which Hitler undoubtedly suffered. The source of the word comes from the ancient Greek, *hustérā*, meaning womb, thus reinforcing the concept of a birth.

SUMMARY

The Third Antichrist will soon be born. His birth will be a disaster for the world.

BIRTH OF THE THIRD ANTICHRIST – PRESAGE II

Laict, sang, grenouilles escoudre en Dalmatie,
Conflit donné, peste pres de Balenne:
Cry sera grand par toute Esclavonie
Lors naistra monstre pres & dedans Ravenne.

Milk and the blood of frogs flows in Dalmatia

Battle is joined, there is plague near Balennes

Wailing will echo throughout enslaved Slovenia

When the monster is born in and near Ravenna.

The second of three presages to quatrain number 3/35 – 2035 [Birth of the Third Antichrist] contains a rather nice reference to one of Aesop's fables. A frog and a mouse decide to engage in single combat to settle the question of who owns the marsh they both live in. With the battle well under way, and their attention concentrated elsewhere, an artful kite then swoops down and carries both combatants off.

Ancient 'Dalmatia' lies almost entirely inside modern-day Croatia, which has traditionally been fought over by the Serbs and the Croats – it hardly stretches the imagination, therefore, to imagine the Serbs as frogs and the Croats as mice, and the Muslim minority, or perhaps even the Russians, as the artful kite? Either way, battle is joined near *Balenne* (which is probably Baleni Romini, in Romania, situated 40 miles north of Bucharest).

The monster, or Third Antichrist, is then born in, or near, Ravenna. It may, at this point, be apposite to point out that as well as the more obvious Ravenna, in Italy, there are also two Ravennas in the country formerly known as Yugoslavia. One, Ravna Reka, is in Serbia, and the other, Ravne na Koroskem, is in Slovenia, which ties in quite nicely with line three.

SUMMARY

The three possible sites of the Third Antichrist's birth are given. Bad luck will come to those countries abutting the place.

BIRTH OF THE THIRD ANTICHRIST – PRESAGE III

DATE

2034

NOSTRADAMUS'S INDEX DATE
34
CENTURY NUMBER
3

Quand le defaut du soleil lors sera,

Sur le plain iour le monstre sera veu:

Tout autrement on l'interpretera,

Cherté n'a garde: nul n'y aura pourveu.

At the total eclipse of the sun

The monster will be seen in broad daylight

He will be misinterpreted

None will have foreseen the great cost.

In 2034 a total eclipse of the sun is expected on 20 March, a little ahead of the sun's transit from Pisces into Aries, the sign of wars, famines, heat, droughts, and magical transformation. The eclipse will pass over central Africa, the Middle East (including Egypt and Iran), and south Asia (including India and China). It will presage the birth of the Third Antichrist [3/35 – 2035], and he will be conceived in the period immediately following the eclipse, and born in the New Year. We know that this is a significant presage because of the paradox hidden within the quatrain, namely that 'at the total eclipse of the sun' (i.e. when all is darkness), 'the monster will be seen in *broad daylight*'. We also know from 2/32 – 2032 that the monster (from the Latin *monstrum* meaning not only a prodigy, or monster, but also an omen, or scourge) will be born either in Italy, Serbia, or Slovenia, all areas well outside the line of the eclipse. His coming will be welcomed by many with secret vested interests, but it will ultimately portend disaster.

SUMMARY

The Third Antichrist is conceived, in darkness, during the total eclipse. He will be born into darkness, too, and he will bring darkness upon the world.

BIRTH OF THE THIRD ANTICHRIST

2035

35

3

Du plus profond de l'Occident d'Europe,

De pauvres gens un ieune enfant naistra,

Qui par sa langue seduira grande troupe:

Son bruit au regne d'Orient plus croistra.

From deep in the Western part of Europe

A child will be born, to poor parents

He will seduce the multitude with his tongue

The noise of his reputation will grow in the Eastern kingdom.

This new leader of the Eastern world will be around 35 years old by the time of the global war referred to in quatrain number 5/70 – 2070. Though only from a humble background in the western Islamic diaspora, he will manage to pull together the equivalent of the old Ottoman Empire by the seductive power of his language, and threaten the dominant positions of the US and China. This will result in a catastrophic nuclear war, 'powerful enough to disturb mountains' [*see* 5/70 again]. The worrying aspect of this quatrain lies in the word '*seduira*', 'to seduce' or 'deceive by charm', in line three, with its implication that this leader will be a manipulator and a fixer, and also in the word '*bruit*', in line four, implying that his reputation will be spun as a form of narrative, rather than fairly earned. It's a worrying quatrain in every respect, and echoes the presage of Adolf Hitler, as the possible second Antichrist, in the now famous quatrain 2/24:

> *Bestes farouches de faim fluves tranner:*
> *Plus part du camp encontre Hister sera,*
> *En caige de fer le grand sera treisner,*
> *Quand Rin enfant Germain observera.*

> With the hunger of wild beasts they will cross the
>   rivers
> Most of the country will be against Hister
> The great man will find himself paraded inside a
>   cage of iron
> The German child (of the Rhine) will see nothing.

This is the closest Nostradamus ever came to a categorical warning to the world about a future potential holocaust, and the subtle language he uses in 3/35 – 2035 echoes this, with its hints of hidden depths and secret manipulations.

Summary

The Third Antichrist is born. The die has been cast. The future of the world, unless a miracle occurs, will be very bleak, with global warfare and ecological damage on an unprecedented scale.

BIRTH OF THE THIRD ANTICHRIST – CONSEQUENCES

2036

36

9

Un grand Roy prins entre les mains d'un ieune,

Non loin de Pasques confusion. coup cultre

Perpet. cattif temps que foudre en la hune,

Lorsque trois freres se blesseront, & murtre.

A great King falls into the hands of a youngster

There is confusion around Easter time, and a knife-blow

Long-term captives, and St Elmo's Fire

At a time when three brothers wound and kill each other.

This is not the only time that Nostradamus uses the image of St Elmo's Fire [*see* 2/90 – 2090: Hungary in Crisis]. He has also used the concept of 'three brothers' before, particularly in 8/46 – 2005 [Death of Pope John Paul II] (both prophecies can be found in my *The Complete Prophecies of Nostradamus*). In that quatrain the 'three brothers' symbolized the Magi, and, given the Easter motif in this quatrain, there is every reason to suppose that he is using the same trope once again. One's instinct is to connect this quatrain with that of the preceding year, 3/35 – 2035 [Birth of the Third Antichrist], and if that is the case, Nostradamus is giving us a second warning.

The 'child born to poor parents' is most definitely *not* the Second Coming, as, in his case, the Magi (figuratively) fall out. The mention of 'Easter time' is an obvious reference to the death of Christ, and this is further strengthened by the mention of a 'knife-blow', which equates with the lance driven into Jesus's side. Given all this, it would appear that the 'great King' in line one refers directly to Jesus, and that it is he, or more correctly his followers, who risk falling into the hands of 'the youngster', causing confusion.

SUMMARY

The Third Antichrist will be declared the Second Coming. This will not be true. He will damage both the world and the Christian Church.

BOOK BURNING

Le Neron ieune dans les trois cheminees

Fera de paiges vifzs pour ardoir getter,

Heureux qui loing sera de telz menees,

Trois de son sang le feront mort guetter.

The young Nero, using three chimneys

Will burn the living word in his ardour

Happy the person far from such practices

Three of his own blood will watch him die.

Part of a trio of quatrains (*see* 4/52 – 2052: Emancipation of Muslim Women and 2/54 – 2054: Monsoon Rains in my *The Complete Prophecies of Nostradamus*) which deal with the restrictive practices put into place by a fundamentalist Muslim State. The number 'three' also arises twice within the quatrain, and is thus significant – Pythagoras even considered it the perfect number, expressive of a beginning, a middle, and an end.

In this case we are dealing with the burning of books deemed blasphemous by the mullahs. 'Nero' was a leader intimately associated with fire, who may or may not, as Roman emperor, have ordered the burning of Rome. At the very least, or so it is alleged, he forbade the putting out of the fire, because he 'wanted to see how Troy would look when it was in flames'. But a 'Nero' is also a generic term for any bloody-minded man, relentless tyrant, or evildoer of extraordinary savagery. Could this young Nero be the now 21-year-old man Nostradamus speaks of in 7/32 – 2032 [Birth of the Third Antichrist – Presage I]? If so the number three would exactly describe his life, and its effect, for as we know from the Bible, 'the enemies of man are threefold – the world, the flesh and the devil'.

The quatrain, too, is in three stages – the 'young' Nero, with his three chimneys; the 'mature' Nero, who burns books; and the 'dead' Nero, killed by 'three of his own blood'. There are, of course, three Antichrists, too. Napoleon, Hitler, and the strangely persuasive gentleman whose birth is announced in 3/35 – 2035 [Birth of the Third Antichrist].

Summary

This is a plea against censorship, and in favour of freedom. The Third Antichrist is building his power base by playing on his followers' greed for power over others, just as Adolf Hitler manipulated his followers through the gift of favours and of political and civic office.

WORLDWIDE EPIDEMIC

Mabus puis tost alors mourra, viendra
De gens & bestes une horrible defaite:
Puis tout à coup la vengeance on verra,
Cent, main, soif, faim, quand courra la comete.

Mabus, though dead, returns

Both man and beast suffer terribly

Then, all of a sudden, vengeance arrives

Much blood, thirst, hunger, when
the comet passes.

'Mabus' is one of the cryptograms most beloved of Nostradamus's commentators. It has been transliterated into just about everything, ranging, in ascending order of lunacy, from Saddam Hussein (via Da Vinci-esque mirror writing), to 'self-abuse', the Magus, Megabyzus, Aenobarbus, Thurbo Majus, Abu Nidal, Abu Abbas, and even as far as poor old Raymond Mabus, former Governor of Mississippi and US Ambassador to Saudi Arabia (1994–6), who found himself in imminent danger of being tarred as either the Third Antichrist, or, worse still, one of his victims, thanks to the efforts of a mixed bag of Nostradamian conspiracy nuts. To be fair, no one claims to have the definitive answer, and many of these suggestions are put forward with tongue solidly in cheek.

In point of fact, Nostradamus's coining of the name Mabus probably stems from something as commonplace as his knowledge of his close contemporary, the Flemish painter Jan Gossaert (1470–1532), who was known as Mabuse after his birthplace of Maubeuge, in France. There may be a connection, too, with the legend of Queen Mab, the fairies' midwife of dreams, the title of Queen referring, not to a regal background, but to the simple fact that she was a woman (equating with the still current Scots word *queynie*, and the no longer current Saxon word *quïn*). So could Mabus simply mean the 'time of dreams'? If that is the case, then the quatrain takes on a haunting, doomed quality, part nightmare and part hallucination. Whatever meaning we construe from it, 2062 sounds like a particularly bad time to be alive.

SUMMARY

An epidemic that was thought to be defeated flares up again, killing many more people than before.

PEACE REIGNS OVER THE EARTH

Les fleaux passés diminue le monde

Long temps la paix terres inhabitées

Seur marchera par ciel, t/serre, mer, & onde:

Puis de nouveau les guerres suscitées.

With the plague over, the earth shrinks

Peace will reign for a good while

People will travel through the sky, like birds, and by sea and wave

Before war once again is called for.

Following the terrible epidemic described in 2/62 – 2062 [Worldwide Epidemic], which has decimated the world population, things will return to normal for a while. There will be peace. Travel will recommence. The word *serre* in line three is of particular interest here, because in Old French it means the 'talon of a bird', giving an image of people travelling through the air as if carried by a hawk – one trusts it's not invidious to remind readers, at this point, that there was no such concept as 'air travel' in Nostradamus's time. Here, he is simply taking it for granted, as if his visions had vouchsafed him a sight of the future which he accepted completely, as if it were an everyday matter.

The war in line four, of course, is the global war due in 2070 [*see* 5/70], and which he warns us about, yet again, in 10/69 – 2069. It is interesting to note that in both this quatrain, and in 10/69, Nostradamus uses the word *seur*, meaning *sueur*, 'by the sweat of one's brow'. The juxtaposition of that word with *serre*, the talon of a bird, is undoubtedly intentional, and implies human, rather than God-like, will, in our mastering of the elements.

SUMMARY

The earth's population has drastically shrunk, thanks to the worldwide epidemic of 2062. There is a period of calm and harmony in the world, possibly as a result of collective shock.

ENGLAND & SCOTLAND FALL OUT OVER EU

Le chef de Londres par regne l'Americh,

L'isle d'Escosse tempiera par gellee:

Roy Reb auront un si faux antechrist

Que les mettra trestous dans la meslee.

London's prime minister, ruled by America

Will freeze out the Scottish enclave

The Rob Roys will pick themselves so false an Antichrist

That they will all be thrown into the mix.

This quatrain is significant for the fact that it specifically mentions the word 'Antichrist' in line three, suggesting a pluralism, rather than merely a singularity of Antichrists – thus reinforcing Nostradamus's concept of a trinity (ergo 6 + 6 + 6). The conflict to which it refers apparently stems from England's secession from the EU (*see* quatrain 8/60 – 2060 in my *The Complete Prophecies of Nostradamus*), and the schism this creates with Scotland, which resolves to remain inside the community. England will align itself with its old ally, the United States, while Scotland will align itself with its 'auld ally', France.

Rob Roy, of course, was the nickname of Robert McGregor, an amiable rogue and a splendid swordsman, who assumed his mother's name of Campbell when his clan was outlawed by the Scottish Parliament of 1662 – it didn't take him very long to become Scotland's equivalent of England's Robin Hood, though, and he only evaded transportation to Barbados by a whisker. This time the Scottish 'Rob Roys' will find that the ally they have picked for themselves is full of perfidy, and leaking with ulterior motives. Is it any coincidence that the index number of this quatrain, 10/66 – 2066, also coincides with the 1,000-year anniversary of the Norman Conquest?

SUMMARY

Scotland and England disagree profoundly over Scotland's membership of the European Union. England sides with the United States over matters of trade, while Scotland sides with France.

WARNINGS OF GLOBAL WAR

Le fait luysant de neuf vieux esleué
Seront si grand par midi aquilon,
De sa seur propre grande alles levé.
Fuyant murdry au buysson d'ambellon.

The shining deed of the newly elected elder

Will be blown south by the great northern wind

Great halls are raised by his own sweat

Fleeing, he is killed at the bushes of Ambellon.

A precursor to the global war scenario laid out in 5/70, 9/70, 2/70, 8/70 and 3/71? The index date is right, and other clues lead us towards such a supposition, most notably the symbol of the 'northern' wind 'blowing south'. Most commentators have always taken '*seur*' in line three to mean *soeur*, or sister, but it is much more likely, if taken as an ideogram, to mean *sueur*, 'sweat'.

'The bushes of Ambellon' remain a mystery. There is a clue, however. Bellona, wife of Mars, was the Roman goddess of war, and temples ('great halls') were traditionally built to her when war was in the offing. In classical literature, too, Bellona soon began to be linked to the moon-goddess of Asia, some time following the Mithridatic wars. The beaten Mithridates, of course, not wishing to fall into the hands of his enemies, found that he had so fortified himself with antidotes against poisoning by others, that he was unable to poison himself, and was finally forced to get a slave to stab him.

SUMMARY

There are rumblings of war, despite the placatory efforts of a newly elected leader.

AN ASTEROID STRIKES THE EARTH

La grand montaigne ronde de sept estades,

Apres paix, guerre, faim, innondation,

Roulera loin abysmant grands contrades,

Mesmes antiques, & grand fondation.

The great mountain, seven stades around

After peace, war, hunger, flood

Will roll far, destroying great swathes of country

Even antiquities, and mighty foundations.

This is an odd quatrain, which seemingly splits into two, because line two strikes one as being a forerunner of the coming, Antichrist engendered, global war, while lines one, three and four describe a precipitating event. Such premonitory events abound in the Bible and in history, and Nostradamus is clearly using a similar conceit here, along the lines, say, of the appearance of Halley's Comet on 24 April 1066, which prefaced the 14 October 1066 Battle of Hastings, and which is clearly delineated on the famous Bayeux Tapestry (*isti mirant stella* – 'these men wonder at the star'), in which Harold of England is seen receiving news of the comet with fear in his eyes.

A '*stade*' was a unit of measurement equivalent to about 180 metres, so a 'mountain seven *stades* around' would measure 1,260 metres in circumference, or 1,377.93 yards. One presumes that Nostradamus is talking about an asteroid strike here, for we know that a 1-km asteroid, travelling at circa 30 km per second, would have a huge impact on all terrestrial life. Tsunamis would be triggered, rising to between 300 and 800 metres above sea level. Firestorms and dust storms would circumnavigate the globe, blotting out the sun for one to two years, and disrupting food chains and breeding cycles. We can expect one such asteroid strike roughly once every 100,000 years, and Nostradamus would seem to be indicating the year 2069 as a possible strike date.

SUMMARY

Nostradamus predicts an asteroid strike in 2069, and describes the likely consequences. It is clear from the quatrain that he sees this is a premonitory even for the global war of 2070.

GLOBAL WAR I

2070

70

5

Des region subiectes à la Balance,

Feront troubler les monts par grand guerre:

Captif tout sexe deu & tout bisance,

Qu'on criera à l'aube terre à terre.

From the regions governed by Libra

A great war will come, enough to disturb the mountains

Both sexes will be captured, and all Byzantium

So that cries will be heard at dawn, from country to country.

If the two countries in the 'Libran' balance of power are the US and China, as Nostradamus clearly established in two of his previous quatrains (1/54 – 2054: US/Chinese Standoff, and 1/56 – 2056: Islam Disturbs the Balance of World Power – *see* my *The Complete Prophecies of Nostradamus*), then 'Byzantium', by which Nostradamus would appear to mean those Islamic countries once comprised within the old Ottoman Empire, will be the ember that lights the flame of global war. The war will be a nuclear one ('powerful enough to disturb mountains'), in which both men and women will fight in combat roles, particularly on the Islamic side. At the end of the war, either lamentations will be heard, or, quite possibly, the call of the muezzin (or 'announcer'), echoing from country to country of the subjected region.

SUMMARY

The war begins, triggered by the Islamic world. The United States and China finally face up to each other on a global arena.

GLOBAL WAR II

2070

70

9

Harnois tranchant dans les flambeaux cachez

Dedans Lyon le iour du Sacrement

Ceux de Vienne seront trestous hachez

Par les Cantons Latins, Mascon ne ment.

Slicing armour is hidden in the torches

Inside Lyon, on the day of the sacred mountain

Those of Vienna will be put in the mincer

By the Latin cantons; Macon does not lie.

A continuation of the global war scenario Nostradamus begins in 5/70 – 2070, and completes in 3/71 – 2071. 'Macon' is Muhammad, the name stemming from the poeticization of the name of Mecca, Muhammad's birthplace, in classical and medieval romance literature, which Nostradamus would certainly have been familiar with. 'Praised (quoth he) be Macon whom we serve.' (Fairfax *trans*: Tasso, xii. 10).

The 'mountain', in line two, is Mount Safa, which did *not*, of course, come to Muhammad: 'If the mountain will not come to Muhammad, Muhammad must go to the mountain.' Goaded on by his followers to produce a similar miracle to those Moses and Jesus were said to have wrought in testimony to their divine authority, Muhammad, irritated by their lack of belief, devised a strategy to bring them to their senses. He called Mount Safa to him, and when it refused to come, he thanked Allah, 'because it would have fallen on us to our destruction'. Here, the implication seems to be that the Western powers have called to the mountain, and it has fallen on them, in the guise of nuclear weapons – 'slicing armour hidden in the torches'. If we cast our eyes back to quatrain 5/70, of course, we also see that the coming great war will be 'enough to disturb the mountains'.

The pun on *Vienna*, and '*de Vienne*', in line three is also a neat one. The Congress of Vienna (1814 to 1815), carved up Europe between the great powers, following the downfall of Napoleon, and the liaison of *de* and *vienne* gives us the French for to 'become' – there will be changes to the established order, therefore, as a direct result of this conflict. It is, perhaps, useful to remember that the four great powers involved in the

Congress of Vienna were Austria (the Hapsburg Empire), Britain, Prussia (the German Confederation), and Russia.

SUMMARY

Thermonuclear weapons are used on the battlefield. Whole mountains are destroyed. Efforts are made at peacemaking, but they are futile.

GLOBAL WAR III

Le dard du ciel fera son extendue,

Mors en parlant: grande execution.

La pierre en l'arbre, la fiere gent rendue,

Brut, humain monstre, purge expiation.

The spear from the skies will complete its
extinguishing

It will speak of death: a terrible execution

The proud nation will be returned to the stone
in the tree

Rumours of a human, brutish monster bring
first catharsis, then sacrifice.

These really are an extraordinary series of quatrains [10/69, 5/70, 9/70, 8/70 and 3/71], all conterminous by index date, and all with implications of nation states brought low by global thermonuclear warfare. Why have they never been linked before? The index dates are categorical, and the symbols used are unequivocal. 'The spear (or dart) from the skies will complete the extinguishing' – a wonderful description of an intercontinental missile, for *estendre* in Old French means to 'stretch', or 'spread', and *esteindre* to 'extinguish' (the s was later replaced by an acute accent). The concept of the 'stone in the tree' means, quite literally, to be returned to the Stone Age, in which axes were made from split branches, with sharpened celts looped in for heft. The 'human monster' takes us back once again to 3/35 – 2035 and the birth of the Third Antichrist (the first two being Napoleon/Stalin and Hitler). The 'seductive' leader would, by 2070, be 35 years old, and in the full flow of his maturity.

S U M M A R Y

The war is nearly over. Unparalleled destruction has been rained upon the world. Entire countries are no more. The Third Antichrist makes his move.

GLOBAL WAR IV

Il entrera vilain, meschant, infame

Tyrannisant la Mesopotamie,

Tous amys fait d'adulterine d'ame.

Terre horrible noir de phisonomie.

He will enter, ugly, bad, and infamous

He will tyrannize Mesopotamia

Friends will pretend that the adulterous one
has a soul

The land is horrible, and black of aspect.

Is this the 'human monster' mentioned in 2/70 – 2070 [Global War III], who will bring 'first catharsis, then sacrifice'? A better description of sycophantic expediency has never been penned than in line three's 'friends will pretend that the adulterous one has a soul'. 'Mesopotamia', of course, is modern-day Iraq, with a little bit of Turkey and Syria thrown in for good measure. Not much seems to be left of this former cradle of human civilization, however, and far from living up to the meaning of its name in Greek as being the land situated 'between two rivers', it now seems more a case of its being the land situated 'between a rock and hard place'.

SUMMARY

The Third Antichrist attempts to benefit from the fallout of the global war. People want to believe him. He makes his power base in what remains of the Middle East.

GLOBAL WAR V

Ceux dans les isles de long temps assiegés

Prendront vigueur force contre ennemis:

Ceux par dehors mors de faim profligés,

En plus grand faim que iamais seront mis.

The islanders will face a long siege

They will defend themselves vigorously

Those outside will be assailed by hunger

It will be a far worse famine than those which
preceded it.

A direct follow-on from 5/70, 9/70, 2/70 and 8/70 – 2070 [Global War], in which the US and China go head to head in a thermonuclear contest. Nostradamus often referred to the British as 'the islanders', and given the contents of 8/60 – 2060: England Secedes From European Union and 8/64 – 2064: Consequences of England's Secession From EU (*see* my *The Complete Prophecies of Nostradamus*) and the implications of a British famine that is only halted by a mass return to the countryside, one could extrapolate from this that the United Kingdom remains apart from the global conflict, reverting to the Fortress Britain role that it played during World War Two.

While war rages on the continent, therefore, Britain becomes self-fuelling, and self-feeding – trusting to the 'spade'. Those outside its borders face a terrible famine, but the United Kingdom, in a bid to save itself and its people, does not let them in.

SUMMARY

Britain has, for once, held itself aloof from the conflict. It now reaps the benefit. While a significant part of the rest of the world goes hungry, Britain has become self-sufficient, and manages to feed its own people.

GLOBAL WAR AFTERMATH/END OF PHOENIX PERIOD

2075

75

2

La voix ouye de l'insolit oiseau,

Sur le canon du respiral estaige

Si haut viendra du froment le boisseau,

Que l'homme d'homme fera Antropophage.

The cry of an extraordinary bird will be heard

Canoning through the air shafts

The cost of a bushel of wheat corn will soar
so high

That man will make of man a cannibal.

Following on from the catastrophic global war of 2070 [5/70, 9/70, 2/70, 8/70 and 3/71], a terrible famine will devastate the earth, triggering the Change of World Order depicted in 3/79 – 2079. Birds such as crows, owls, storks, ravens and swallows were considered harbingers of either good or evil (depending on breed, colour and connotation) by the augurs of ancient Greece, but Nostradamus's use of the phrase *'insolite oiseau'* would seem to point us towards a rarer bird – the phoenix, for instance. For Paracelsus, the phoenix symbolized alchemy, on account of the animal's ability to change its essential form through the use of fire, and for centuries the sign of the phoenix was to be found above pharmacies and chemists' shops for that very reason.

Phoenix periods (when the phoenix is actually visible to human beings) range from 250 years, according to Tacitus, to a maximum of 1,500 years between sightings, according to the German Egyptologist Lepsius. Such sightings were deemed to herald the beginnings and ends of great human eras. If we take the length of a phoenix period to be around 300 years, as is now generally acknowledged, we are taken back to 1775, and the start of the American War of Independence, an event that heralded both the beginnings of world revolution and the foundation of modernity. This period, Nostradamus tells us, is now at an end. Instead, we are entering a period of barbarism, rather than enlightenment – a period of uncertainty and global change.

SUMMARY

The war has signalled the end of a great human era. Everything will now change. We are entering a period of barbarism and immorality, on an unprecedented scale.

THIRD ANTICHRIST I

2075

75

10

Tant attendu ne reviendra jamais

Dedans l'Europe, en Asie apparoistra

Un de la ligue yssu du grand Hermes,

Et sur tous roys des orientz croistra.

The eagerly awaited one will never return

To Europe, but will reappear in Asia

One of the confederacy descended from great Hermes

He will grow above all other kings of the Orient.

One immediately thinks of the series of quatrains dealing with the period 2032–36 [Birth of the Third Antichrist], when one reads this prophecy. The individual concerned, whose birth is described so effectively in 3/35 – 2035, would be 40 years old at the time of this quatrain. It seems that he has survived the global war of 2070, and is intent on proving Nostradamus's prediction in 3/35, that 'the noise of his reputation will grow in the Eastern Kingdom', correct – this suggestion is echoed in line four of the present quatrain, in 'he will rise above all other kings of the East'.

As if that weren't enough, we are reminded of his European origins [*see* 2/32 – 2032], and are now told that he repudiates them totally, and turns his face permanently towards the East. The 'confederacy descended from great Hermes' is of particular interest here, as it could imply an Hermetic link with Thoth (the Egyptian Hermes Trismegistus, scribe of the gods, and chief councillor to Osiris). Either that, or a reference back to alchemy, for Hermes was the Greek Mercury, and Milton, in *Paradise Lost*, iii, 603, calls quicksilver 'volatile Hermes'. In purely classical terms, Hermes was the god of thieves, as well as messenger and herald to the Olympians, and he was also the conductor of souls to Hades. On the whole, though, it seems most likely that Nostradamus was taking the Neo-Platonist route, as the name Trismegistus means 'thrice great', and we are dealing here with the man who may well be the Third Antichrist.

SUMMARY

This is the time the Third Antichrist has been waiting for. From the Middle East, he moves towards Asia, widening his power base.

THIRD ANTICHRIST II

L'antechrist trois bien tost annichilez,

Vingt & sept ans sang durera sa guerre,

Les heretiques mortz, captifs, exilez,

Sang corps humain eau rogie gresler terre.

The Third Antichrist will soon be annihilated

His war will have lasted for twenty-seven years

The heretics are either dead, captive, or exiled

Human blood reddens the water that covers the earth in hail.

Could the war Nostradamus is describing really have started in 2050, when the Third Antichrist was a mere 15 years old? [*see* 3/35 – 2035: Birth of the Third Antichrist]. Well, yes, it could, if the war is accepted as being one of ideological, rather than of military confrontation. There is no question here of the war having actually come to an end, but the presage in line one may link this quatrain to 3/79 – 2079 [Change of World Order], in which the example of the men of Phocis is summoned up to show that all is not yet lost. The final line is one of the greatest, and yet most difficult to translate, in all of Nostradamus's writings, and conjures up, in its few, almost shunted-together words, a human- and nature-driven hell the like of which we haven't experienced since the last great Quaternary Ice Age of 1.6 million years ago. The original source of the image of 'blood reddened' hail comes in Revelations 8. vii, and describes the first of the seven angels of God: 'The first angel sounded, and there followed hail and fire mingled with blood...'

SUMMARY

There are still some people willing to fight back against tyranny. Nostradamus describes the battle and suggests that, in the end, the Third Antichrist will be beaten.

FORTRESS BRITAIN FOLLOWING GLOBAL WAR

2077

77

2

Par arcs feuz poix & par feux repoussés:
Cris, hurlements sur la minuit ouys
Dedans sont mis par les remparts cassés
Par cunicules les traditeurs fuis.

By arcs of fire, pitch, and flame are they repulsed

Screams, cries, and shouts at midnight

They are launched from inside the smashed
defences

The traitors escape through their
secret passages.

One is tempted to see this as a continuation of the prediction from 3/71 – 2071 [Global War V], in which the UK becomes Fortress Britain once again. There is certainly the sense of a siege here, which would make sense if Britain had become self-sufficient in food, and others wished to benefit from its bounty. It seems that the British drive off the invaders, at a terrible cost, and fifth columnists and traitors escape by the very underground passages through which they sought to undermine their own people.

SUMMARY

Britain defends its borders, and its right to isolation, against outsiders. Fifth columnists inside the island fail in their treason.

CIVIL DISOBEDIENCE BEGINS

2078

78

10

Subite ioye en subite tristesse

Sera à Romme aux graces embrassees

Deuil, cris, pleurs, larm. sang excellent liesse

Contraires bandes surprinses & troussees.

Sudden joy inside sudden sadness

Will occur at Rome, of the jealously guarded favours

Mourning, cries, tears, weeping, blood, excellent joy

Opposing groups surprised and locked up.

This is a quatrain of paradoxes. 'Sudden joy inside sudden sadness'. 'Mourning, cries, tears, weeping, blood', and then the unexpected use of the Old French word '*liesse*', which also means joy. 'Opposing groups', which one takes to mean groups on both sides of the argument, are 'surprised and locked up'. This is almost a judgment of Solomon, when one comes to think about it – the sort of response a State will give if it finds itself at an impasse, facing two opposing sides who will not, under any circumstances, compromise. What Nostradamus is describing, therefore, is the beginnings of tyranny under the guise of political expedience, which, in the light of 3/79 – 2079 [Change of World Order], will come as no surprise whatsoever.

SUMMARY

All over the world, parameters are changing. Former democratic states are arrogating despotic powers to themselves. There are mass insurrections, which are put down pitilessly.

CHANGE OF
WORLD ORDER

2079

79

3

L'ordre fatal sempiternel par chaisne,

Viendra tourner par ordre consequent:

Du port Phocen sera rompue la chaisne:

La cité prinse, l'ennemi quand & quand.

The locked and fated eternal order of things

Will switch direction, thanks to a new order

The old Greek order will be broken,

Its citadel taken; the enemy will not be accepted.

Given what Nostradamus predicts in the years both leading up to, and following, this quatrain, its meaning becomes all the more pivotal. It is rare for Nostradamus to generalize to such an extent, and it can only mean that he is uncertain as to the true outcome of events. Given all that, he appears to foresee what amounts to a fundamental change in the perception of democracy ('the old Greek order'). Could its 'citadel' be Athens? Or is that too literal a reading?

The 'new order' (tyranny?) does not, at the very least, find easy acceptance. Phocensian despair, of course, means desperation which terminates in victory, and stems from the days of Philip, King of Macedon, when the men of 'Phocis' (*see* line three in the French) stood alone against the united might of all their enemies. In desperation, they built an enormous pyre, meaning to immolate themselves, and their women and children, upon it. Having nothing left to lose, they then threw themselves in one final, despairing act, upon the foe, and, extraordinarily, beat them off.

SUMMARY

The old world order has changed, apparently for good. Democracy is a thing of the past. There are many, however, who regret its passing. Having nothing left to lose, they ready themselves for one last-ditch attempt at a restoration of universal suffrage. Extraordinarily, and against all the odds, they are successful, igniting the beginnings of a new, more positive era.

CLIMATE CHANGE DUE TO GLOBAL WAR

2080

80

8

Des innocens le sang de vesue & vierge.

Tant de maulx faitz par moyen se grand Roge

Saintz simulacres tremper en ardant cierge

De frayeur crainte ne verra nul ne boge.

The blood of innocents, of widows and virgins

The great Red One commits many evils

Holy images are infused with the light of
votive candles

Terrified and fearful, people will no longer
dare to move.

Following on from the Global War of 2070 [*see* 5/70, 9/70, 2/70 & 8/70 – 2070], great climatic change will come upon the world. The French, at the time Nostradamus writes, held the belief that a 'red man' (red was also the colour of the devil) commanded the elements, wrecking those he condemned to death somewhere in the seas off the coast of Brittany. Legend also has it that this same 'red man' once appeared to Napoleon in a dream, foretelling his downfall. The 'Red One', therefore, is Nostradamus's euphemism for the elements, which run amok in the aftermath of a thermonuclear war, making any form of travel impossible, and rekindling, as so often happens in times of turmoil, a return to organized religion. The restoration of a communal faith was a continual preoccupation of Nostradamus's, and he returned to the subject time and time again in his writings.

SUMMARY

Fundamental climate change, triggered by the thermonuclear war of ten years back, begins to tell. People turn back to God in their uncertainty. After the horrors of an entirely man-made war, nature is now poised to take its revenge.

TSUNAMI I

2080

80
4

Pres du grand fluve, grand fosse terre egeste,

En quinze pars sera l'eau divisee:

La cité prinse, feu, sang, crys, conflict mettre,

Et la plus part concerne au collisee.

Near the great river a ditch will form; the land will be eaten

The water will split into fifteen channels

The city falls; fire, blood, and cries conflict

Much of it caused by the collision.

When taken with 8/80 – 2080 [Climate Change Due to Global War], and 1/82 – 2082 [European Earthquakes], the 2080s do not seem like a good period to be living in southern Europe. The implication of '*collisee*' in the last line gives us both a 'collision', and the geographical location of the Coliseum, in Rome. A 'great river', the Tiber, runs through Rome, and Rome is situated just 17 miles from the Tyrrhenian Sea. The Tyrrhenian Sea contains Europe's largest underwater volcano, Mount Marsili, which rears up 9,800 feet from the ocean floor. Mount Marsili was, until recently, considered dormant, but it has now been firmly established (since 1999) that the volcano is active. When Mount Marsili eventually erupts, as it most certainly will, a considerable part of the southern coast of Italy will go with it. With this in mind, quatrain 4/80 takes on a new, and far more sinister, dimension.

SUMMARY

An underwater volcano erupts beneath the Tyrrhenian Sea, causing a tsunami, which devastates the Roman peninsula.

TSUNAMI II

2081

L'oiseau royal sur la cité solaire,

Sept moys devant fera nocturne augure:

Mur d'Orient cherra tonnairre, esclaire,

Sept iours aux portes les ennemis à l'heure.

The royal bird will fly over the city of the sun

Seven months earlier there will be a
nocturnal augury

The Eastern wall will fall, amidst thunder
and lightning

For seven unremitting days the enemy will be
at the gates.

This is a direct follow-on from 4/80 – 2080 [Tsunami I], and shows just how cunningly Nostradamus linked the numbers of his quatrains and their meaning, despite their nominal appearance in entirely different *Centuries*. In this case the link is not only through the index numbers of 80 and 81 respectively, but also in more subtle ways.

Nostradamus mentions the 'city of the sun', in line one. This was traditionally seen as Rhodes, whose tutelary deity the sun was – its great Colossos, one of the seven wonders of the ancient world, was consecrated to Apollo, god of the sun. This quatrain, with its hidden echoes of 4/80, takes the environmental disasters which befall southern Europe between the years 2080 to 2082, even further south.

The 'royal bird' is the ibis, sacred to Egypt, a country situated just 400 miles due south of Rhodes – to kill one was a capital offence. The implication here is that both Rhodes and Egypt are linked in an environmental catastrophe, whose origin stems from the shattering of the 'Eastern Wall'. The fallout from the catastrophe will continue for 'seven' days, just as the augury occurred 'seven' months earlier, and just as there were 'seven' wonders of the ancient world, which included the Colossus, and 'seven' wonders of the Middle Ages, which included the Coliseum. 'Seven', of course, is a holy number, and Levitical purifications, of which this tsunami may be seen as one, traditionally lasted for 'seven' days.

SUMMARY

Another tsunami devastates the Aegean area around the island of Rhodes, causing havoc on the Turkish mainland.

NEW LEADER APPEARS

Le grand criard sans honte audacieux,

Sera esleu gouverneur de l'armee:

La hardiesse de son contentieux,

Le pont rompu, cité de peur pasmee.

The great scolder, bold and shameless

Will be elected head of the army

The boldness of his contentions

Will cause the bridge to break and the city to faint with fear.

This quatrain comes bang in the middle of three terrible years in which the world order changes, and in which nature, twisted and suborned by man to his own ends, finally wreaks its revenge upon the earth. This period throws up a special sort of leader – a man who harangues and scolds his people until they finally elect him head of the army. It is natural for people to seek strong leadership at a time of uncertainty, and this man provides that leadership. Coming so soon after 3/79 – 2079 [Change of World Order], this quatrain could almost be viewed as an optimistic one, despite the worrying implications in the last line. With what nature has in store for the world, firm leadership will become a necessity.

SUMMARY

A brash new leader, who is, nonetheless, benevolent, comes to the fore. People, searching for miracles, turn to him. He is only a man, however, and cannot turn back the clock.

EUROPEAN EARTHQUAKE

Quand les colomnes de bois grande tremblée

D'Auster conduicte couverte de rubriche

Tant vuidera dehors grande assemblée,

Trembler Vienne & le pays d'Austriche.

When even the trees shake mightily

And the south wind seems covered in blood

So many will try to escape

That Vienna and all Austria will shake with
their passing.

Nostradamus's use of the word 'shake' on two separate occasions in this quatrain gives us our clue. An earthquake, of a sufficient magnitude to make even the greatest trees tremble, will strike central Europe, with its epicentre possibly near, or inside, the Czech Republic. The western part of the Bohemian Massif is well known for its earthquake swarms, with more than 8,000 separate quakes recorded in the period between 1985 and 1986, just 100 years before Nostradamus's predicted date for the big one. The dust from the quake will filter and transform the sun's rays until they seem 'covered in blood', and there will be a mass exodus on such a scale that even 'Vienna', situated a scant few kilometres from the Czech border, will 'shake with their passing'. When, in addition, we take into account quatrain 8/80 – 2080 [Climate Change Due to Global War], with its index date of 2080, the pattern begins to fall even more firmly into place.

SUMMARY

Natural disasters, triggered by the global war, continue. An earthquake strikes the Czech Republic. Its power is so great that aftershocks are felt across the Austrian border.

LOCUST PLAGUE

Freins, Antibol, villes au tour de Nice,

Seront vastees fer, par mer & par terre

Les sauterelles terre & mer vent propice,

Prins, morts, troussés, pilles sans loy de guerre.

Fréjus, Antibes, and the towns around Nice

Will be devastated both by land and by sea

Locusts will come on propitious winds

Kidnap, death, rape, pillage, no martial law.

More natural disasters for this apocalyptic three-year period (2080–82). If anyone ever doubted that Nostradamus's quatrains were linked across the different *Centuries* in which they appear, then the last few predictions, all relating to natural disasters, and all occurring within three years of his index dates in *Centuries 8, 4, 5, 1* and *3*, should convince them otherwise. The Mediterranean, to put it bluntly, is in for it. Tsunamis, earthquakes, climate change – all contrive to create a new environment, a new landscape, almost, in which the coastal borders of Europe are perpetually at risk.

In the bare few lines of this quatrain, an entire story emerges of dreadful storms, followed by a plague of locusts, followed by a total collapse of law and order, in which people go, quite literally, mad, and only the strong, or the wicked, can survive. It comes as no surprise to find that, just three years after these events, the French State is entering a long-term period of crisis [10/85 – 2085].

SUMMARY

Climatic conditions trigger a plague of locusts, but on an unprecedented scale. The French Riviera is particularly hard hit when the locusts are borne over from North Africa on freak winds.

US EARTHQUAKE

2083

83

9

Sol vingt de taurus si fort terre trembler.

Le grand theatre rempli ruinera,

L'air, ciel & terre obscurcir & troubler,

Lors l'infidelle Dieu & sainctz voguera.

When the sun is at 20° in Taurus, a great earthquake

Will totally destroy the packed Great Theatre

Air, sky, and earth will be murky and unsettled

So that even Infidels will call on God and the saints to steer them.

The years 2080 to 2084, encapsulated in an index-conjoined series of quite remarkable quatrains, seem among the bleakest that mankind will ever have to go through. Earthquakes, tsunamis, locust plagues, and radical climate change will harry the world as a result of our own actions, and there will be a mass return to organized religion [*see* 8/80 – 2080: Climate Change Due to Global War].

The next Jupiter in Taurus square to Neptune in Leo will occur in 2083. The last occurred in June 1929, a few months before the great October Wall Street Crash, which ushered in a ten-year period of unmitigated disaster for all the Western economies, and, in particular, for the United States. Nostradamus speaks specifically here of a terrible earthquake which will destroy what he calls the 'Great Theatre'. Could the 'Great Theatre' be Wall Street?

SUMMARY

Parts of New York are destroyed by an earthquake. The fall of the great buildings creates such a dense pall of smoke, dust, and debris, that for a long time the rescue and emergency services find it impossible to function.

AFTERMATH OF THE COMING OF THE THIRD ANTICHRIST

Naistra du gouffre & cité immesuree,

Nay de parents obscure & ténébreux:

Qui la puissance du grand roi reveree,

Voudra destruire par Rouan & Evreux.

He will be born of the pit and of the immeasurable city

Product of dark and infernal parents

Who wish the power of the great and revered king

To be destroyed by Rouen and Evreux.

This would appear to be yet another Third Antichrist quatrain, with a probable date of 2084 – the wording is so severe, and the reference to the infernal regions so specific, that it appears to be a natural follow-on to the sequence of disasters foretold in the quatrains describing the years 2080–4, and predates the French Crisis sequence that starts in 2085.

SUMMARY

Another in the infernal chain of quatrains describing the catastrophic years 2080–4.

FRENCH CRISIS PRELUDE I

Le vieil tribung au point de la trehemide

Sera pressee captif ne deslivrer,

Le veuil non veuil ne mal parlant timide

Par legitime à ses amys livrer.

The old demagogue, with the salt measure
teetering

Will be urged never to release the captive

The old man, though not weak, does not wish
to be maligned

By legitimate means he delivers him to his friends.

Quatrain number 10/98 – 2098 [French Crisis I], in my *The Complete Prophecies of Nostradamus*, deals with the symbolical significance of 'salt', both as a concept of the vigour of the State, when the salt is kept neatly sealed up, and as an evil omen, when it is spilled or wasted. This quatrain predates that one by exactly 13 years (13 is an unlucky number – traditionally, in the city of Paris, no house bears it – it was also the number present at the Last Supper, in which Judas upset the salt shaker), and points to what may have caused the French crisis in the first place.

'*Trémie*', in Old French, is a mill-hopper, or salt measure, and also carries with it the implication of shaking, which is generally seen as an adjunct to old age. *Vieil*, *veuil* and *veule* mean, respectively, 'old', 'wishes' and 'weak', all, once again, leading us towards the image of an elderly leader, without vigour, unsure of his ground, and minding overmuch what is said about him. The identity of the mysterious 'captive' is a moot point, but it is perhaps apposite to point out that the Third Antichrist spoken of in 3/35 – 2035, would be just 50 years old at the time of this quatrain.

SUMMARY

A crisis has been brewing in France. Now it comes to a head. The aged leader hesitates, uncertain how to respond. This is a fatal mistake.

TWENTY YEARS SINCE END OF GLOBAL WAR

Les dieux feront aux humains apparance,
Ce qu'ils seront auteurs de grand conflict:
Avant ciel veu serein espée & lance,
Que vers main gauche sera plus grand afflit.

It will seem to human beings that the gods

Must have been the authors of the great war

Once, long ago, the sky was clear of weapons

Whereas now, on the left hand, there is damage
still to come.

It is now 20 years since the end of the 2070-1 Global War [5/70, 9/70, 2/70, 8/70 & 3/71], and the long-term fallout, both emotional, ecological, and thermonuclear, is still being felt. The war was so terrible that its seems to many observers as if non-human forces must have been involved in its inception. People look back nostalgically to a serene time when the skies were clear of hardware and tactical weapons, and, presumably, full of birds. Nostradamus would have had no concept of the existence of either a left or a right wing in terms of politics, but he would have known, from his reading of Plato, Plutarch and Aristotle, that the 'left' was the side of evil omens and of sinister actions, and that any signs seen over the left shoulder were considered particularly bad auspices by the Greek and Roman augurs, who reputedly studied the flight of birds for signs of future trends.

SUMMARY

Twenty years after the end of the global war, the great powers come together at a conference to consider its implications for the future of the planet. People regret the passing of the old days, and fear that further conflict is imminent.

ECOLOGICAL BURN-OUT

2095

95

2

Les lieux peuples seront inhabitables:

Pour champs avoir grand division:

Regnes livrés à prudents incapables:

Lors les grands freres mort & dissension.

Formerly inhabited lands will become unfit for
human life

Cultivatable fields will be divided up

Power will be given to overcautious fools

From that moment on, death and discord for the
great brothers.

The 'great brothers' are *Liberté*, *Égalité* and *Fraternité* (Freedom, Equality and Brotherhood), symbols of the revolutionary French Republic, and known historically as the Declaration of the Rights of Man and of the Citizen. This would tend to link the quatrain to the French crisis of 2098–2101, which Nostradamus predicts in a sequence of quatrains (*see* my *The Complete Prophecies of Nostradamus*), except that the verse would seem to point towards an ecological, rather than an overtly political, crisis. It's possible, of course, that the land reform mentioned in line two forms part of the fuse that eventually triggers the constitutional upheaval, but the global nature of line one might incline us to veer away from a purely parochial reading. Line three is a stunner, and could be applied to almost all governments and their incumbents, and is surely worthy of use as a one-off epigraph in its own right.

SUMMARY

The ecological fallout from the global war of 2070 continues, with swathes of the world left virtually uninhabitable. The quality of leadership, though, in the aftermath of the crisis, leaves something to be desired.

THE MIDDLE EAST

2097

97

3

Nouvelle loy terre neufve occuper

Vers la Syrie, Iudee, & Palestine:

Le grand empire barbare corruer,

Avant que Phebés son siecle determine.

New laws will rule new lands

Towards Syria, Judea and Palestine

The great barbarian empire will decay

Before Phoebus concludes his dominance of
the century.

'Phoebus' is the sun. In Greek mythology Apollo was called Phoebos, the sun god, after the act of shining. He was regarded as the font of moral excellence, and his influence was a benevolent one. The implication here is that moral and ethical laws are overturned in the Middle East, and I am tempted to refer back to 2/85 – 2085 [The Future of Israel] in my *The Complete Prophecies of Nostradamus*, for a possible explanation of what has occurred. The 'great barbarian empire' is possibly that of Israel, therefore, when one takes into account the meaning of the word 'barbarian' in its biblical sense (and we are talking of the Bible lands here). 'Therefore if I know not the meaning of the voice, I shall be unto him that speaketh a barbarian, and he that speaketh shall be a barbarian unto me.' (I Corinthians xiv. 11.)

Yet another reading could have the Arab world as the barbarian empire, with both sides refusing to understand each other, or to hear each other's voice. A third reading gives us the word barbarian in its literal, and Latinate sense, as the 'bearded one'. German legend has it that Charles V, with his crown and sceptre, and with all his knights and vassals surrounding him, still lives inside the Wunderberg, on the great moor near Salzburg, haunt of the Wild-women. His grey beard has twice encircled the royal table, and when it grows long enough to encircle it three times, the Antichrist will appear.

SUMMARY

The Middle East remains tinder dry, and cracks are appearing in the entrenched positions of both parties.

THE GREAT COMEDIAN

7073

73

10

Le temps present avecques le passé

Sera iugé par grand Iovialiste,

Le monde tard lui sera lasse,

Et desloial par le clergé iuriste.

Time present and time past

Will be judged by the great comedian

The world will tire of him when it is too late

Having forsaken its conventional clergy.

With its index date of 73, and its apocalyptic content, this is clearly a run-up to Nostradamus's End of Days quatrain, number 10/74 – 7074: Armageddon/The Final Prophecy. The poet, T S Eliot, obviously had the present quatrain in mind when he wrote as the opening lines to Burnt Norton (Number 1 in the Four Quartets]):

> Time present and time past
> Are both perhaps present in time future,
> And time future contained in time past.
> If all time is eternally present,
> All time is unredeemable.

Nostradamus's sensational image of the 'great comedian' also tallies with his End of Days quatrain, for lines one and two of 10/74 read: 'When the great number seven completes itself/Games will begin at the Tomb side.'

Here he foresees the run-up to Armageddon as reflected in the loss of mankind's interest in 'conventional' religion. Enlightenment, as always, comes too late, and the 'great comedian' (whom we may reasonably assume to be Satan), snatches the pot.

Summary

Human beings have forsaken religion in favour of pleasure and instant gratification. The devil has won. In the next quatrain Nostradamus imagines Satan cutting a caper at the side of mankind's universal tomb.

ARMAGEDDON/
THE FINAL PROPHECY

7074

74

10

Au revolu du grand nombre septiesme

Apparoistra au temps ieux d'Hacatombe,

Non esloigné du grand eage milliesme,

Que les entres sortiront de leur tombe.

When the great number seven completes itself

Games will begin at the Tomb side

Not far from the turn of the Millennium

The dead will rise out of their graves.

'Seven' is the holy number, and equates, symbolically, with a span of length – the beginning and the end of things. Just as there are seven ages in the life of man, and seven bodies in alchemy, and seven spirits of God, so there have been seven great eras in the life of the earth. These are now over.

Nostradamus's use of the word *'jeux'* (games) in line two is an odd one, but then we remember the Greek concept of the playfulness of the gods (*see* 8/16 – 2016: Ecological Disasters II in my *The Complete Prophecies of Nostradamus*), and the image is no longer so surprising – it is echoed, too, in his image of the 'great comedian' in the previous quatrain [*see* 10/73 – 7073: The Great Comedian].

The final dating of Armageddon presents some difficulties, as we do not know if Nostradamus is dating his 7,000-year span from the inception of Man, or from the birth of Christ. Either way, the world is moving inexorably towards its end, and the sum total of our human achievements will be neither significant, nor remembered, in its aftermath.

SUMMARY

The final joke is on us. Everything humanity thought would last will be lost in the mists of time. We are simply part of a whole, and relevant, even to ourselves, no longer. The great comedian has won.

SUMMING UP

C G Jung, in his *Answer to Job*, echoes Nostradamus's final two quatrains almost perfectly: 'The end of the world is, however, preceded by the circumstance that even Christ's victory over his brother Satan – Abel's counterstroke against Cain – is not really and truly won, because, before this can come to pass, a final and mighty manifestation of Satan is to be expected.' Jung goes on to explain that 'one can hardly suppose that God's incarnation in his son Christ would be calmly accepted by Satan. It must certainly have stirred up his jealousy to the highest pitch and evoked in him a desire to imitate Christ (a role for which he is particularly well suited as the *antimimon pneuma*), and to become incarnate in his turn as the *dark* God.'

Jung takes his image of the *antimimon pneuma* – the 'counterfeit spirit', if you will – from the Apocryphon of John III, 36:17. The Apocryphon, or Secret Book of John (*see* my epigraph at the front of the book), is a key Gnostic text, belatedly rediscovered at Nag Hammadi in Egypt in 1945. In it, the Godhead is construed as potentially dualistic, a view which ties in perfectly with Antichristian symbolism, and which may reasonably be taken as having influenced much later eschatological theory.

Nostradamus, too, was well-versed in Gnostic theory, and appears to have had no problem at all with the mirror concept that darkness, by definition, presupposes light, and good, evil. If one takes this view to its logical conclusion, the existence of God would, by definition, presuppose Satan, and the existence of Christ, would, by default, suggest an equal and opposite Antichrist.

So what are the principal constituents of Nostradamus's Antichrists? We have firm evidence for at least two of them, after all, and may we not reasonably extrapolate from this towards a third?

Both Napoleon and Hitler were, for a start, transnational – e.g. their influence and desire for expansion extended beyond their own borders to around the world. They were transformational – e.g. their main desire was to manipulate and alter the status quo. They were anti-clerical – e.g. they could not stomach moral competition. They were totalitarian – e.g. democracy was anathema to them. They encouraged personality cults – e.g. they wished to place themselves before God in the minds of the people. They came 'from the people' – e.g. they wished to appeal to the lowest common denominator and did not feel that they could do this if they were seen as stemming, or owing their power to, an elite or an aristocracy. Despite this, both still created secret elites, often mimicking older established elites, and to which they alone controlled the access – e.g. they understood that to properly control their subordinates, they had to secure their loyalty through lucrative advancement. They reused old models of chivalry – e.g. they hoped to benefit from archetypal thought modes and thus short-circuit and reuse established chains of command. They dominated the military, for they realized that therein lay the swiftest route to total power. They had delusions of grandeur, in that, soon after taking power, both started to believe their own publicity, with Napoleon being crowned Emperor, and Hitler allowing himself to be known as 'the leader'. Both were obsessive self-justifiers, in that both were fundamentally incapable of accepting that they might be wrong about anything.

In addition both were small men – I don't mean this pejoratively, but in the sense of small of stature – possessing, as a concomitant, super-large egos. Both were possibly subject to psychosomatic illness. Both were allegedly manic depressive, and both may possibly have contracted syphilis at some point in their lives. Both were obsessed with numerology and the occult and the belief that secret, esoteric knowledge might imbrue its possessor with total power. Both were obsessed by dress, uniform, and outward show. Both had favourites. Both were outsiders, and thus, perhaps inevitably, preoccupied with cultural identity and with belonging. Both attempted to dominate the arts, to the extent that both instigated artistic movements and strangled or outlawed other movements that did not suit their world view.

It's an extraordinary picture, and one which quite possibly predicts the character of the 'One Still to Come'.

We'll give Jung the final word. As he says in his *Aion*, such men encapsulate 'a false spirit of arrogance, hysteria, woolly-mindedness, criminal amorality, and doctrinaire fanaticism... they are purveyors of shoddy spiritual goods, spurious art, philosophical stutterings, and Utopian humbug, fit only to be fed wholesale to the mass man of today. That is what the post-Christian – [*ergo Anti-Christian*] – spirit looks like.'

SELECTIVE BIBLIOGRAPHY

Anderson, Sir Robert, *The Coming Prince: The Marvellous Prophecy of Daniel's Seventy Weeks Concerning the Antichrist* (London 1881 – reprinted Cosimo Classics 2007)

Bunyan, John, *Of Antichrist and his Ruin* (London 1692)

Cruden, Alexander, *A Complete Concordance to the Old and New Testament or a Dictionary and Alphabetical Index to the Bible* (Frederick Warne and Co., Ltd., of London and New York. 1737–69)

Emmerson, Richard Kenneth, *Antichrist in the Middle Ages: A Study of Medieval Apocalypticism, Art, and Literature* (University of Washington Press 1981)

Fuller, Robert, *Naming The Antichrist: The History of an American Obsession* (Oxford University Press USA, 1996)

Hill, Christopher, *Antichrist in Seventeenth-Century England* (Oxford University Press 1971)

Istrin, V, *The Apocalypse of Methodius of Patara and the Apocryphal Visions of Daniel in Byzantine and Slavo-Russian Literature* (Moscow 1897)

Jung, C G, *Answer to Job* (Routledge & Kegan Paul, London, 1954)

　Aion (Routledge & Kegan Paul, London, 1959)

Lake, Peter (with Michael Questier), *The Antichrist's Lewd Hat* (Yale University Press, 2002)

Lorein, G W, *The Antichrist Theme in the Intertestamental Period* (T & T Clark, 2004)

McGinn, Bernard, *Visions of the End* (Columbia University Press, 1998)

   Antichrist (Columbia University Press, 2000)

Nietzsche, Friedrich, *The Antichrist* (1895). Translated by H L Mencken

Pink, Arthur, *The Antichrist: A Systematic Study of Satan's Counterfeit Christ* (Bible Truth Depot, Pennsylvania 1923)

Preuss, H, *Die Vorstellungen vom Antichrist im späteren Mittelalter, bei Luther u. i. d. Konfessionellen Polemik* (Leipzig 1906)

Prophet, Elizabeth Clare, *The Path of Christ or Antichrist* (Summit University Press 2007)

Richardson, Joel, *Antichrist: Islam's Awaited Messiah* (WinePress, 2006)

Riddlebarger, Kim, *The Man of Sin: Uncovering the Truth about the Antichrist* (Baker Books 2006)

Russell, Jeffrey Burton, *The Prince of Darkness: Radical Evil and the Power of Good in History* (Cornell University Press, 1992)

Schütz, Paul, *Der Antichristus* (1933, Gesammelte Werke/Collected Works, 1963)

Schütze, Alfred, *The Enigma of Evil* (Floris Books, 1978)

Thompson, Damian, *Waiting for Antichrist: Charisma and Apocalypse in a Pentecostal Church* (Oxford University Press USA, 2005)

Upton, Charles, *The System of Antichrist: Truth and Falsehood in Postmodernism and the New Age* (Harper Collins 2005)

Wadstein, E, *Die eschatologische Ideengruppe, Antichrist, Weltsabbat, Weltende und Welgericht* (Leipzig 1896)

Williams, Stephen N, *The Shadow of the Antichrist* [Nietzsche's Critique of Christianity] (Baker Academic, 2006)

INDEX